THE SERVANT WARRIOR LEADER

Phil Johnson,
MBL Coach

Master *of* Business Leadership

Library and Archives Canada
Cataloguing in Publication

Johnson, Phil, 1953-

The servant warrior leader : mastering authentic business leadership / Phil Johnson.

ISBN: 978-1-897453-56-8

1. Leadership. 2. Success in business. I. Title.

HD57.7.J645 2007   658.4'092   C2007-905315-7

Cover photo: With kind permission of: Nelson Harrison, Photographer Medieval Faire - Chatham

We acknowledge the financial support of the Government of Canada through the Book Publishing Industry Development Program (BPIDP) for our publishing activities.

Printed and bound in Canada. Published October 15, 2007

Manor House Publishing Inc. 452 Cottingham Crescent, Ancaster, Ontario, Canada, L9G 3V6   (905-648-2193)

www.manor-house.biz   Email: mbdavie@manor-house.biz

Contact information for the author:

Phil Johnson, MBL Coach, Silicon Synergy Inc

Bus: 905-272-5690   Cell: 416-729-7445

MBLCoach@MasterofBusinessLeadership.com

MasterofBusinessLeadership.com

MasterofBusinessLeadership.blogspot.com

Next time you are out for a walk, pick up a hand full of dirt. As you examine it, hear the words that Emily Dickinson composed over 100 years ago.

THIS quiet Dust was Gentlemen and Ladies,
And Lads and Girls;
Was laughter and ability and sighing,
And frocks and curls.
This passive place a Summer's nimble mansion,
Where Bloom and Bees
Fulfilled their Oriental Circuit,
Then ceased like these.

By Emily Dickinson, 1830-1886

There Is One Underlying Truth In This Book And In Life –
Be Who You Are And Inspire Others To Do The Same

Free Coaching Session!

Master of Business Leadership Coaching Program –
Even Strong Leaders Can Achieve Greater Results!

The Servant Warrior Leader and the Master of Business
Leadership coaching program were written and created
to help companies and individuals get better results.
The MBL program is a unique and brilliantly straightforward approach to leadership that will raise your
awareness of what may be holding you back and help
you strive to be the only servant warrior leader you
should ever be waiting for – You!

We offer a complementary coaching session
with each Servant Warrior Leader book.

To find out more, please contact:

Phil Johnson, MBL Coach
http://www.linkedin.com/in/executivecoach
MBLCoach@MasterofBusinessLeadership.com
Bus: 905-272-5690

Contents

Getting Better Results

I am certain you will enjoy Phil's book and interacting with him through the MBL program as much as I did. His concepts have already helped us close $500,000 in business.

- Joanne Moretti, General Manager & SVP, US West

Finally a no-nonsense program designed to transfer the skill to achieving better results. Unproductive, perceptions and habits are replaced with more productive and more frequent results.

- Hal W. Keiser, CEO Profit Quest Inc

If Abraham Lincoln were alive today he would be trumpeting this book and the MBL Program. Many of the tools and insights that he discovered and used during the course of his life are very consistent with what's offered in this program.

- Jeff Hayward, Vice President Marketing, Global Fortune 500 Software Company

I regard Phil as one of the most innovative thinkers and problem solvers on the planet today! Any organization that hires Phil will get a ten-fold return on their investment!

Derrick Sweet, CEO, Healthy Wealthy and Wise Corp.

Acknowledgments

To my wife and best friend — Brenda, your love and encouragement has always inspired me to be who I am.

To my dad, Fred "Buck" Johnson — *To thine own self be true.* You were right.

To Sam and Eric - The freedom to choose, to direct your lives, is your most precious gift and power.

To Manor House Publishing and Michael B. Davie for bringing my work to the masses. Thank you.

Many thanks to the companies and individuals that have allowed me the honour and privilege of being their *Master of Business Leadership* Coach. As emerging Servant-Warriors, the leadership and courage you demonstrate is a constant source of inspiration. I am very grateful to my family, friends, colleagues, advisors and others — your love is an amazing gift.

Throughout history, authentic leaders have continued to inspire others long after their deaths. The legacy of their life's work may actually have taken on more significance for us as we have grown and developed. Leaders of the past have left us incredible messages because they wanted to connect with and serve not only current, but also future generations. They knew their lives would not be long enough.

The 21st Century's global economy has shown us that our lives and actions are more interconnected than ever before. My intention is that these tools and insights will serve to inspire both individuals and businesses to take action and become truly authentic leaders.

WE ARE THE ONES WE'VE BEEN WAITING FOR

Editor's Note

Over the past three months, I have worked one-on-one with Phil Johnson, and I can honestly say that as a Leadership Coach, he is at the top of his game. Phil helped me to overcome writer's block, enabling me to complete my own manuscript for publication.

By working through the habits, perceptions and fears that were holding me back, I was gradually able to develop the confidence to pursue an entirely new and more rewarding career path. Phil is truly a Master of Business Leadership Coach!

Rarely does one have the opportunity to work on a manuscript that is brimming with gems of wisdom. I told Phil early on that his work contains so much densely packed information, it could actually be expanded into an entire series. While this book will help you get started, I encourage you to consider obtaining your own MBL, and experience a truly remarkable business and life transformation.

— Lisa Summers, Editor and author
Men Are Like Mocha Lattes

A Word From the Publisher

With *The Servant Warrior Leader*, Phil Johnson has encapsulated what true leadership is all about: An authentic leader motivates, inspires and empowers others to take leadership responsibility for themselves individually to achieve results that are profoundly rewarding to both the individual and the organization. A true servant warrior leader selflessly serves the leadership process and facilitates the innate desires and leadership abilities of others to do the best job possible. The servant warrior leader brings out the best in others.

At the same time, the servant warrior leader is indeed a warrior, playing a champion role in marshalling the leadership talents of others. Simply put, the servant warrior leader is a general of generals, a leader of leaders firmly focused on achieving worthy goals on a short and long-term basis, conquering fears and overcoming limitations to unleash the leader in all of us.

Phil Johnson will change the way you think. He'll change your approach for the better - and he'll help you develop the leader within you.

Michael B. Davie, author, *Winning Ways* series.

Foreword:

Discovering 'Authentic Leadership'

There is nothing in the world that has a more profound impact, for better and worse, than leadership. Leadership in all its dynamic forms represent in real terms one of the most significant factors in determining the successes and failures of human beings. Yet, many see leadership from an internal locus of control, something one exercises upon others, something that exists to fulfill the need to manage, direct, and organize people toward a common goal.

Nothing could be further from the truth. Real leadership, in its most effective form, inspires and motivates people. It's what leadership coach Phil Johnson terms in his Master of Business Leadership program (MBL) as 'authentic leadership'. To celebrate one's unique and authentic self, with the goal of serving and inspiring others - this is possibly the most liberating discovery a developing leader can make. Authentic leadership is self-empowering - yielding greater personal and organizational results.

The idea of being true to oneself is not new, Shakespeare penned about it long ago. But our world's modern day leadership often reflects yesterday's approach as we struggle to shake the leadership hangover from the past. By overcoming the fear that breeds victims within us, and by rejecting the power-based win-lose "carrot and stick" leadership that much of our world is still unconsciously practicing, we can begin to be true to ourself. That's the point when authentic leadership naturally takes hold. Even strong leaders could be achieving greater results by simply focusing on inspiring others which in turn raises the level of engagement of every employee and team member. The payoff is huge.

What does authentic leadership look like and how is it different?

Good leaders motivate people to become high performers and achieve goals both individually and collectively. Good leaders are able to neutralize or diffuse conflict and transform it into a positive force moving in a focused direction toward the goal. They also have a stabilizing effect in an organization during turbulent times. And good leaders are usually always strong communicators. But today that's simply the employment prerequisite in many organizations. What Phil Johnson's coaching program makes alarmingly clear is that even consistent high achievers can often be leaving results on the table because they may be missing out on several critical ingredients. Honesty and compassion are two of them that can make an overwhelming difference.

An example of a 'master' of authentic leadership

Authentic leadership isn't some kind of "strategy du jour" for modern leaders, it has always existed. It's not a societal construct cooked up by a management consultant or business school. It's all around us, but most of us just aren't aware of it. And, as Phil points out, that's because nobody told us, "we don't know what we don't know". But looking closely at well known leaders in history, we can spot some of the truly successful ones who developed an ability to empathize, who sought to first understand rather than be understood, and who always maintained a strong value system that was transparent and respected.

Abraham Lincoln is a standout. There are many in our past that are revered on coins and monuments, and this doesn't necessarily mean they were particularly great leaders. Lincoln however, was a master and embodied all the elements of an exceptional leader. He may be one of the few political leaders in the world whose words, actions and results even to this day act as an inspirational example of the best leadership can be. In my view, Lincoln was great because he possessed the critical traits of honesty, compassion, and a 'people' approach to results.

He seemed doomed to fail - shortly before he took office in 1861, the southern states seceded from the US federal Union. He was perceived as an awkward inexperienced lawyer from a small constituency. Many predicted he would be the last U.S. President. Yet he achieved such enduring results when so much seemed stacked against him. Through the years of conflict that marked the American civil war, Lincoln always practiced a degree of honesty that cemented his reputation as a man with the highest level of integrity and fairness (his moniker was "Honest Abe"), and it provided him a great degree of leeway with his critics when he needed it, and an incredible loyalty from his governing team as well as ordinary citizens who might have otherwise lost faith in him and the Union.

In addition to his honesty, historical accounts widely note Lincoln possessed a remarkable compassion and empathy for all, even for those that he privately acknowledged perhaps didn't deserve it. He always gave people the benefit of the doubt, even his underperforming generals and his opposition that frequently attacked him. To be sure, he was a highly results oriented man, he held those around him accountable but never personally took responsibility for their own actions, he left that to them, empowering and encouraging them where necessary but clearly articulating what was expected every step of the way. And it's Lincoln's sense of empathy and understanding that paved the way for his place in the history books. At the end of the civil war, the issue of the South's fate was hanging in the balance. Lincoln avoided the mistake that so many in history before and after had made. He didn't publicly persecute the Confederate leaders, nor did he penalize and hold down the South through punitive trade and governing restrictions, instead he began a long healing and unification process by making the South a stakeholder in the nation. Lincoln was not vindictive in the least, he knew that people always want to know how much you care, and he made frequent and genuine efforts to show it.

Like all good leaders, Lincoln was ultimately all about results. But he knew results come from people, not memos and directives. Authentic leaders view results as a direct derivative of strong people relationships. For Lincoln people always came first, results were simply something that were produced when they're truly empowered, inspired and motivated. Lincoln spent a great deal of time out of the White House and in the field meeting with commanders, citizens, civic leaders and others. It's one of the reasons he's widely viewed as having been a 'man of the people'.

If Abraham Lincoln was alive today he would be trumpeting the MBL Program. Many of the tools and insights that he discovered and used during the course of his life are very consistent with what's offered in this program.

What I love most about Phil Johnson's MBL program

Awareness of what's holding you back

Phil's program helps to peel back the layers of how we look at ourselves and others and it reveals, in Phil's words, the "many stories we tell ourselves". These self-fulfilling stories are fuelled by the fear, habits and perceptions that we individually harbour but which we are mostly unaware of. Once we become aware of those fears, habits, and perceptions, as well as the walls we build around ourselves as a result, there ceases to be an excuse for anything less than full engagement in all aspects of our lives. It's amazing how many stories I was telling myself, and now I find I'm calling myself on it. It's this level of awareness of what's truly holding us back that helps pave the way for incredible results that all of us are capable of.

The wood/heat syndrome

The MBL program promotes a basic and powerful philosophy: 'If you want more, give more'. I love this, it's really tied into the concept that teamwork and relationships can't be 'conditional', and it turns 'carrot and stick' management on its head. Phil talks about how the "I'll give you wood if you give me heat" syndrome doesn't work - by giving the wood rather than asking for heat, conflict often melts away and forward momentum is sustained. I have personally embraced this approach and it has had a significant impact on several relationships where I now feel a breakthrough has truly been achieved.

The toxic leader

At some point in our careers we all have or will likely come into contact with the 'Toxic Leader'. This is the person who is so old school and wrestling internally with so much fear that they simply poison the organization with their habits and actions. Yet they survive. It would be easy simply to avoid these people, but often we have no choice but to face them. By lowering our own walls and focusing on what's really important, we become authentic and it's the best way to engage the toxic leader. It frustrates them of course, they want desperately to steal everyone's energy and encourage others to also become the victims that they already are. These types usually leave the organization once the culture turns against them, but until that happens they act as an obstacle to achieving high performance results. The MBL program better prepares you to deal with the 'toxic leader' by helping you first avoid becoming a victim of your own self, and also preparing you from becoming a victim of those who masquerade as real leaders.

Most people all want to have an impact within our organizations and communities. The truth is that results come from people, and people that are fully engaged deliver better results. Engaged people are those that are highly motivated and truly inspired by authentic leadership. Phil Johnson's MBL program is a unique and brilliantly straightforward approach to leadership that will raise your awareness of what may be holding you back and help you strive to be the only servant warrior leader you should ever be waiting for - You!

Jeff Hayward
Vice President, Marketing
Global Fortune 500 Software Company

Introduction

It's time for me to write this book. I am 53 years old. It seems to me that just as soon as my freckles went away, my hair went grey. Life is a gift, and if we aren't careful to show up for every moment, it can all too quickly pass us by. I often talk to my clients about the importance of creating intentions and taking *action*; this book is the result of my own intention to write an inspirational call-to-action.

The search for external power has created the fear that sets individuals and corporations against each other. It is the same struggle that creates conflict and wars. It is the same struggle that set Cain against Abel. All of our social, economic and political institutions reflect our understanding of power as external. We are in a time of deep change. We will move through this change more easily if we are conscious of the road on which we are traveling, our destination and what it is that is in motion.

This book and the Master of Business Leadership program were created to assist in that awareness. There is a growing need for individual and organizational leadership. By developing our authentic leadership we connect with our internal power as individuals and organizations leading to greater alignment and synergistic results. This is not a "how to" book. If these articles and contents inspire you to take action, then the MBL Coaching Program may be your next step.

Most people would be hard-pressed to describe what authentic leadership really is or what it looks like.

We are so exhausted by the daily challenges of working and living that we have little time, energy or interest in such reflections. What's more, we were never taught to be leaders by our parents, teachers or employers because nobody taught them. *They didn't know what they didn't know.*

You are perfect (really).

Our habits, fears and perceptions have created the "walls" that blind us to our perfection. We need better leadership to obtain better results. It begins with the stories we tell ourselves.

We have evolved as far as intellect will take us. As a species, we are moving from the view and pursuit of power and leadership as external to the pursuit of authentic internal power and leadership. From Five-Sensory (IQ) to Multi-Sensory (IQ, EQ, SQ) humans. We are becoming conscious of our perfection.

True Leadership Is Not About *Changing* Who You Are — It's About *Being* Who You Are

The Real 21st Century Capital —
It's You

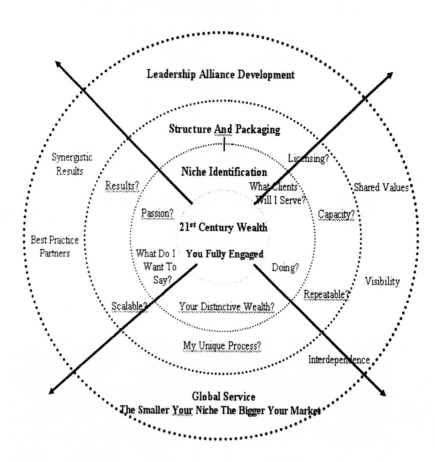

It's All
About You!

You are the true currency of the 21st Century. Money is simply a medium of exchange, a measure of value, and a means of payment. In the 21st Century, the economic currency is you and your people. A recent Gallup survey placed the current level of employee engagement at a mere 29 percent. Furthermore, according to a recent survey by Badbossology, a majority of employees spend 10 or more hours per month complaining or listening to others complain about bad bosses — and almost one-third spend 20 hours or more per month engaged in this activity. If you are part of this majority, ask yourself the following: *Do my actions reflect those of a leader, or a victim? Do they characterize someone who is moving forward in life, or someone choosing to remain stuck?*

Imagine that you are standing in front of a large fireplace with your arms full of wood. Using someone else's actions to justify your lack of engagement is like saying to that fireplace — *I'll give you wood when you give me heat.* In other words, disheartened by others' failure to give, we often stubbornly refuse to give of ourselves, resulting in a frustrating stalemate. The answer, as you'll learn, isn't to stop giving: it's to give *more.* Your level of workforce engagement is your choice, regardless of the circumstances.

Truly authentic leaders have the ability to arouse "discretionary energy" in others. Their leadership serves to inspire others to want to contribute more — they don't use "position-based power," nor do they use a "carrot or stick" approach. They simply demonstrate the strength and courage to be *themselves*, and so inspire others to do the same. A cursory review of some of today's most inspiring leaders reveals an interesting common thread: Bill Gates, Oprah Winfrey and Nelson Mandela all have one thing in common: the ability to inspire others through their *actions.*

The real wealth of the 21st Century is in people. We

need to break with the industrial control model of the 20th Century that treats chairs, buildings and land as assets and people as expenses. People are the true assets. Nowadays, almost everyone feels tremendous pressure to produce more for less. At the same time, the vast majority of people are not being allowed to use their talents and capacities to the fullest potential within their companies. There is profound disempowerment and alienation of people in organizations. The reason: we are still using the old industrial age paradigm during the current information age. This fundamental incompatibility has created unprecedented levels of employee apathy.

We are living in a global economy that is more interconnected than ever before. Company CEOs, Boards of Directors and "C Level" Managers (i.e., CEOs, CFOs, CIOs) are being paid more than ever. They are also being expected to deliver more than ever. A Booz Allen Hamilton study found the average tenure of a CEO has declined from 7 to 4.6 years. In today's economy, decisions have to be made quickly and they have to be right. Senior executive insecurity has been increasing across the board. Executives are realizing that the command and control skills that got them to where they are will not get them to where they need to be in the global marketplace.

How can successful people get even better? Ironically, their incredibly positive self-image may actually be getting in the way. It may be coloring their view of the current reality, which in turn may be affecting results. Authentic business leadership begins with an honest assessment of how things are today, not how we would like them to be. Too often, people in companies find it difficult to focus on things other than bottom line results. We need to develop and nurture our human capital. We cannot invest on Monday, and expect to make money by Friday! Leadership development is associated with long-term profitability but the corollary is that it is also associated with long-term investment.

Average companies are typically chasing 317 various priorities at any given time. Above-average companies chase just 21.

In order to produce successful results, leadership development must include the alignment of resources within companies and between clients, partners and suppliers.

BECOMING A "SERVANT WARRIOR"

The development of authentic leaders is ultimately your key advantage in the marketplace. Leaders come in all shapes and sizes. The truly authentic leader is a "Servant-Warrior": A unique blend of personal humility and professional will. Servant-Warriors have the courage to accurately perceive their own current realities. They also have the urgent need to move in the direction of better results. They take *action* and in the process confront the fears, habits and perceptions that stand in their way. The battles they fight are internal conflicts even though they may have been triggered by external events. The personal victories and the lessons learned move them towards greater understanding. Looking inward provides the answers and insights that allow them to become inspirational servants.

They seek to be who they are, and recognize their interconnectedness with others.

By resisting being who you truly are, you become vulnerable. By becoming vulnerable you discover your invulnerability.

REFLECT

Can you identify the Servant-Warriors in your business? Do you have any? Does your company encourage and support individuals willing to challenge themselves to develop their leadership?

Leadership Integrity

Integrity is the alignment of what you think, say and do. This definition applies to both individuals and corporations.

Effective leadership development systems are crucial to the enduring success of any organization. It takes time and commitment to develop leaders. Yet, investors over the past decade are demanding near-instant returns. This has placed tremendous pressure on executives to sacrifice long-term growth for immediate gains.

In a related Harvard Business article it was reported most companies do not have to motivate their employees — they have to stop *de-motivating* them. The majority of employees are quite enthusiastic when they start a new job. But in about 85 percent of companies, research finds employees' morale sharply declines after their first six months and continues to deteriorate for years afterward. That finding is based on surveys of about 1.2 million employees at 52 primarily Fortune 1000 companies from 2001 through 2004.

The fault lies squarely at the feet of management — both the policies and procedures companies employ in managing their workforces and in the relationships that individual managers establish with their direct reports. A major reason that so many managers do not assist subordinates in improving their performance is simply, that they don't know how to do this without irritating or discouraging them.

TOWARDS AUTHENTIC LEADERSHIP

Most people would be hard pressed to describe what authentic leadership really is or what it looks like. We are so exhausted by the daily challenges of working and living that we have little time, energy or interest in such reflections. What's more, we were never taught to be leaders by our parents, teachers or employers because nobody taught them. *They didn't know what they didn't know.*

It is a mistake to believe understanding something is the same as knowing it. If you know it and you don't do it — you don't really know it.

Take extremely good care of yourself every day. This is where leadership begins. The development of authentic leaders is one of the greatest challenges of the 21st Century. It requires living a life that reflects more of *you*, your values and your deepest desires. In today's world, many people live with a sense that something is missing. They feel that they have lost part of themselves in the daily madness of their busy lives.

Remember: You are perfect. There is nothing missing. The rest of your life can be the best of your life. It's your choice — it always has been.

Servant Warrior Leader Habits

1. Communications – Turn Fear-Based Responses Into Leadership
2. Listening – Don't Take It Personally
3. Teach People To Fish – Responsible To But Not For Others.
4. Confidence – Take Action >>> Fears, Habits, Perceptions
5. Strategic Action – Do What Is Difficult While It Is Still Easy
6. Engagement – Your Level Of Engagement Is Your Choice – Play Fully Engaged
7. The Results Cycle – Leaders Know That There Are Only Results (The Penny Doubling)
8. The Purpose Driven Life – YDV x Q
9. The Law of Attraction And Quantum Vision
10. The "Right Fit" Delegation System
11. Wealth Creation And Alignment – It's What People Want
12. The Power Of Now – Live Today Like It Is The Last Day Of Your Life (Not The First)
13. Emotional Intelligence: Self-Awareness The Key Leadership Attribute
14. Authentic Energy Protection – PEMS Balance
15. Authentic Sales Leadership: Courage To Close The Solution–Value Gap

Corporations Need To Bring Back The One Room Schoolhouse

What lessons can businesses learn today from the tiny schoolhouses of yesteryear? At one point, the landscape was dotted with them. One of the greatest challenges teachers faced in the one-room era was that they had to educate across many grade levels and subjects, from basic addition to Shakespeare's dramas. But there was an inherent benefit in having so many grade levels in one room.

While there may have been only one formal 'teacher' in the room, there were, in effect, many more, thanks to the older kids who could instruct the younger ones. Also of benefit was the fact that because there were no hard "lines" between grade levels, the students could be coached to their ability and potential.

The advent of the production assembly line in 1913, combined with the institutionalization of education, reduced this level of individual involvement and bonding. The 20th Century saw the creation of "managers" who viewed employees as balance sheet expenses instead of organizational assets. Many years later, it comes as no surprise that we are in the midst of a global leadership crisis and that a recent Gallup Poll survey places the current level of workforce engagement in North America at a mere 29 percent.

The roots of authentic leadership and coaching began in these one-room schoolhouses. Perhaps the most important lesson of all is that relationships are formed one on one, often in small ways and often in small places. Today's best companies are, on close inspection, a collection of one-room schoolhouses whose whole is greater than the sum of its parts.

Who Am I?

More Testimonials...

Often the barriers to success are those we create through attitude or self-limiting habits. Phil Johnson's approach helps individuals get back to the natural strengths and optimism we began with and to make these our new habits and perceptions. The impact is greater personal results, and an energy and attitude to become more effective coaches and enablers of others. The multiplying effect can have significant results for any team; business, sport, or family.

Barry Papoff, VP Engineering, VPD
Harris Broadcast Communications

Working with Phil I discovered my fears, habits and perceptions limit my overall perspective by erecting barriers between myself and others. Only by stripping away these obstacles, could I understand leadership is not something to be exercised but is truly serving and inspiring others to strive for higher performance. Understanding who you are is the first step in becoming an authentic leader.

Bill Wiersma, National Sales Manager
EMA Design Automation

The World
Isn't Flat

You and I are living in a particular paradigm that determines what we can and cannot accomplish. People who lived in the 1400s believed that the world was flat. Similarly, people in the early 1950s believed an individual was incapable of running a mile in less than four minutes. Since Roger Bannister broke the record on May 6, 1954, over 964 people have accomplished the same feat.

What will people say about our beliefs 50 or 100 years from now? We see the world through the tinted glasses of our own paradigm and we are blind to its nature. On average, 50% of our paradigm is in place by the age of five. By age eight, it's about 80% and by the age of 18 approximately 95% of our belief system is in place. We were taught the rules, habits and beliefs of our paradigms by our parents and teachers because they wanted us to survive and be happy.

So why aren't we happy? Why do we sometimes feel inauthentic? Why do we have this feeling that we are pretending to be something we're not? It's because a lot of the paradigm that we accepted as children is simply not true.

> We shall not cease from our exploration, and at the end of all our exploring, we shall arrive where we began and know that place for the first time. — T.S. Eliot

We are living in a very interesting time. Individuals and companies are coming to an increasing awareness that almost everything we think we know is wrong. This is creating incredible opportunities as well as dangers. The future isn't what it used to be.

In this environment of rapid change, success can no longer be modeled by what worked for us in the past. It does not matter what people think about you or your company — what matters is how they feel about the *experience*. It is the experience that must be differentiated. The emotion of the experience leads to action.

Companies need to move from product telling to story telling.

THROUGH THE LOOKING GLASS: MOVING BEYOND OUR CURRENT PERCEPTUAL LENS

There are several actions you can take to become aware of, and move through, your habits, perceptions and fears. A good starting point is to improve your listening skills. One of the most powerful ways that you can become a better listener is by making a conscious effort *not to take things personally.* Often during conversations, something being said triggers us to go into a "survival mode" habit. We feel we are being attacked. A belief, perception or past experience may cause us to unconsciously filter what is being said, and we react.

Yet, when we become immune to others' thoughts, opinions and actions, we actually become more focused, relaxed, connected, effective and happy. This does not mean that you give up responsibility for your actions. What it does mean is that you stop taking responsibility and reacting to the actions of others. What others say or do is never about you — it's about them, their point of view — their reality. By allowing ourselves to look at the thoughts, opinions and actions of others more objectively, we become better listeners. Is this easy to do? Of course not. Is it effective? Yes!

By not taking anything personally, we begin to lower our walls and open up to other possibilities. We step out of our paradigm and begin to see things as they truly are — the true reality. We become both a participant and a curious observer within the conversation. By resisting the urge to react, we demonstrate authentic leadership. Over time, our actions will inspire others (clients, employees, business partners and family members) to do the same.

You Are Not Your Mind

Feel More — Think Less

WE HAVE BECOME
ADDICTED TO THINKING

Not being able to stop thinking is a dreadful affliction. To be who we are in this moment is the goal. Being who we are inspires feelings of interconnectedness, alignment

Our body is not who we are — it is only the vehicle we travel in. Every cell in our body is replaced within each 7-year period – yet we remain. – Wayne Dyer

> It is a mistake to believe understanding something is the same as knowing it. If you know it and you don't do it — you don't really know it. — Phil Johnson

and ultimately, better results. We are separated from being who we are by our habits, perceptions and fears. The stories we tell ourselves that justify not being who we are. Identification with just our minds creates filters, labels and judgements that separate who we think we are from who we really are. This can lead to feelings of separation, isolation and disease. Our minds are just a tool. Who we are has much more to do with how we feel than what we think.

The Universe Is Made Up of Vibrational Energy

We have evolved as far as intellect will take us. As a species, we are moving from the view and pursuit of power as external to the pursuit of authentic internal power. From Five-Sensory (IQ) to Multi-Sensory (IQ, EQ, SQ) humans. We are becoming conscious of our perfection.

The universe consists of both the Physical Universe that we can experience (conscious) with our five senses, and the Quantum Universe we are unable to experience (unconscious) through our physical senses.

Our brain wave vibrations are constantly broadcasting and receiving information. The conscious brain (Beta Waves) makes up 17% of its mass. This part of the brain receives approximately eleven million bits of information per second (BPS), of which we are able to process about 2,000 BPS.

The unconscious brain (Alpha, Theta and Delta Waves) makes up 83% of its mass. This part of the brain receives 400 Billion BPS and controls 96-98% of our perception, behaviour and actions. It also filters our consciousness and can create "blind spots" or scotomas. Next time you see a FedEx logo try to find the arrow in the picture — if you do not readily see it you are experiencing a scotoma. This is an example of the filters that our unconscious mind can create. *We do not see everything there is to see — only what our brain allows us to see.*

Delta   0.1–3 Hz   Deep sleep, lucid dreaming, increased immune functions, and enhanced healing.

Theta	3–8 Hz	Deep relaxation, meditation, increased memory, stress management.
Alpha	8–12 Hz	Light relaxation, "super learning" … access to sub-conscious mind.
Low Beta	12–15 Hz	Focused mental processing, improved attentive abilities.
Mid-Range Beta	15–18 Hz	Increased mental ability, focus, alertness, IQ.
High Beta	18–30 Hz	Fully awake, normal state of alertness.

OUR "BLIND SPOTS"

FedEx

Can You See The Arrow In This Logo?

We Do Not Always See Everything There Is To See —
Only What Our Brain Allows Us To See

Universe
E = MC² Everything Is Energy Vibration

$$E = MC^2$$

Physical Universe   **Quantum Universe**

Physical Universe	Quantum Universe
Five Sensory	*Multi-Sensory*
Humans — IQ	*Humans — IQ, EQ, SQ*
(Experience With	(More Than Just
Our Five Senses)	Our Physical Senses)

We Are Evolving From The View And Pursuit Of Power
As External To The Pursuit Of Authentic Power

BRAIN WAVE VIBRATIONS BROADCAST AND RECEIVE INFORMATION

Conscious	Unconscious
17% Brain	83% Brain
11 Million bps	400 Billion bps
(2,000bps)	Controls 96-98% perception, behaviour, action
	"Blind spots" (Scotomas) filters our consciousness
Beta — Alert, conscious mind	**Alpha** — Relaxation, superlearning, intuition
	Theta-REM sleep, universal intelligence
	Delta- Dreamless sleep, rejuvenation

Changing Our Unconscious Perceptions, Habits
And Beliefs Will Change Our Results

Action   Leader/Victim Awareness/Choice
Individual And Organizational Healing

Law Of Attraction — What You Focus On Expands

Changing our unconscious perceptions, habits and beliefs can change our results. The connection to the universal intelligence in the Quantum Universe is through our unconscious mind. We have the ability to attract the people and resources we need to succeed. By taking action, we can change the story we tell ourselves. Change your brain, and you will change your results.

Know Thyself — to know how other people behave takes intelligence, to know yourself takes wisdom.
— Lao Tzu

By being in the world but not of the world you are both a participant and objective observer.
— Phil Johnson

This above all: to thine own self be true, and it must follow, as the night the day, thou canst not then be false to any man. — William Shakespeare

When you talk with Phil about business leader-ship, his energy and passion fill the room. The active interaction with Phil gave me confidence to believe than we can all be leaders, and I've been passing on the same message within my organization. As a result, I'm seeing others inspired to contribute more. You will experience the same with his book, You Are A Perfect Leader! (Really). Phil is the Master of Business Leadership!

- Ken Williams, VP Professional Services

Authentic Leadership Is Wealth

This article is about how to create wealth which is not the same thing as money. You can have wealth without having money. If you had a machine that could make anything you wanted, you would not need money. The disadvantage of looking at money as wealth is that it obscures what business really means. People think that what a business does is make money. But money is just the intermediate stage - just shorthand for whatever people want. What most businesses really do is make wealth - they do something people want.

There is an infinite amount of wealth in the world and a fixed amount of money at any moment. Money is merely something we use to move wealth around. Although there is a fixed amount of money

available to trade for things we want, there is not a
fixed amount of wealth. We can make more wealth.
Even kids know they can create wealth. If they want to
give someone a present and do not have money, they
make one. A software programmer can sit down in front
of a computer and create wealth. A good piece of software is, in itself, a valuable thing. Employees work
together to create wealth which earns money.

Gallup has estimated the current level of workforce
engagement at creating wealth is 29 percent. Employees
have lost their interest in working together to create
wealth. Position-based power "leadership" that many
businesses use has created victims and low levels of
workforce engagement. The development of authentic
leadership is the solution. It creates both personal
wealth and inspires synergistic organizational wealth
creation within the company. More than 75 percent of
wealth created today is service related. The intangible
capital (patents, R&D, services, etc.) of the world's
largest 150 companies has been estimated at $7.5 tril-
lion - up from $800 billion just a decade ago. Authentic
leadership is wealth - it's what people want and companies need.

Our Energy Compass

$$(E = MC^2)$$

Our energy level is the *compass* that we can use to help us better understand our choices. The decisions that we make or avoid daily either add to or reduce our energy. Decisions that result in increased energy are in line with

> **Between stimulus and response is a space. In this space lies the freedom to choose our response. In these choices lie our growth and our happiness. Next to life itself, this self-awareness and our freedom to choose, to direct our lives, is our most precious gift and power.**

the distinctive value we offer others. Clarity, convic-
tion and awareness develop over time as our energy
increases.

The frequency of our energy increases as we develop
our authentic leadership. Actions that reflect our
authentic self are of a higher frequency than those of
victim activities.

*Everything you are "for" strengthens you — everything you
are "against" weakens you.* — Phil Johnson

Listening —
Don't Take It
Personally

Here is the key to effective listening — *don't take anything personally.*

Often during conversations, something being said triggers us to go into a "survival mode" habit. We feel we are being attacked. A belief, perception or past experience may cause us to unconsciously filter what is being said and we react.

When you become immune to others' thoughts, opinions and actions you become more focused, relaxed, connected, effective and happy. This does not mean that you give up responsibility for your actions. What it does mean, is that you stop taking responsibility and reacting to the actions of others. What others say or do is never about you — it's about them, their point of view — their reality. By allowing ourselves to look at the thoughts, opinions and actions of others more objectively we become better listeners. Is this easy to do? Of course not.

> *We are constantly teaching people how to treat us.*
> — Phil Johnson

By not taking anything personally, we begin to lower our walls and open up to other possibilities. We step out of our paradigm and begin to see things as they truly are — the true reality. We become both a participant and an observer within the conversation. By resisting the urge to react, we demonstrate authentic leadership. Over time, our actions will inspire others (clients, employees, business partners and family members) to do the same. As business leaders, we can experience the awesome power of authentic leadership.

> We are always alone but we are only lonely if we do not like the person we are alone with.

The Evolution Of Power

Throughout history, position-based power leaders have seen power as external. They have looked to acquire and hoard power and have lived in fear of losing it. Conflict and competition were created to compete for this external power. These "leaders" often felt isolated and effectively, un-empowered.

Authentic leaders of the 21st Century see power as internal within themselves and their organizations. Authentic power is *real* power. The individual lessons we learn, by taking action help us to develop our authentic power. We begin to recognize our global inter-connectedness. Compassion, wisdom, grace, and calmness radiate from within once we align our thoughts and actions to create synergistic results.

> *There is a huge benefit in having a professional to guide us on the path to success. Michael Jordan had his coach, Phil Jackson. I have my coach, Phil Johnson. As a public speaker and leadership trainer, I have facilitated over 1,200 leadership trainings to over 35,000 people in the United States, Canada, Panama and New Zealand. I help large groups focus on what they want and how to get there ... but that is just the first step. HOW to get there is one thing ... but actually getting there is another. Phil is a master guide on the path to success.*
>
> – James "Ross" Quinn, President

Intellectual
And Emotional
Capital

The ultimate 21st Century product and service is *you*. The experience and wisdom you offer an employer, client or business partner, can help them to address dangers, opportunities and strengths. When you combine your abilities and resources in a way that increases theirs, you create value for them. When you use your abilities to solve a problem for someone or enable them to capture an opportunity, you earn a level of trust and respect, and the relationship deepens. This allows you to create even more value.

The more you are able to develop and package your unique intellectual property (IP), the greater your potential market. As you become your market niche, your market becomes global. Stop trying to sell commodity products and services that will always face pricing and competitive pressures. Becoming the authentic leader you are will guarantee your market position.

Remember, the greatest value you can offer the marketplace is *you*.

The things to do are the things that need doing — that you see need to be done and that no one else seems to see need to be done. Then you will conceive your own way of doing that which needs to be done — that no one else has told you to do or how to do it. This will bring out the real you that often gets buried inside a character that has acquired a superficial array of behaviors induced or imposed by others on the individual. — Buckminster Fuller

We Learn To Be Victims

During a recent television interview I was asked if leaders are born or created. I responded that we are all born into the world as blissfully unconscious leaders. Living in the present moment - days seemed like weeks and weeks seemed like years. Soon afterwards our highly passionate feelings of connectedness and innocence were disrupted. The reason, unfortunately, is that most of us live in a win-lose model that government has often referred to as a "zero sum game" - where there needs to be a winner and a loser.

By the time we are five years old approximately 50% of our belief system is in place. At eight it is about 80% and this increases 95% by the age of eighteen. We see the world through the tinted glasses of our own paradigm and we are blind to its nature. Struggle and conflict ensues as our understanding of power as internal is replaced by the search for external power. All of our social, economic and political institutions reflect this understanding of power as external.

By developing our authentic leadership we reconnect with our internal power as individuals and organizations. This leads to greater alignment and synergistic business and personal results. The blissful leadership of childhood is replaced by the respect, courage, confidence, intuition and balance of self leadership mastery. Leadership is a choice not a position - it's your choice.

It's Spring —
Time To Plant The
Seeds!

Did you know that when you put a seed in the ground, the first direction it grows is inward and downward to develop a strong root system? A seed cannot sustain its life if it grows upward and forward first. Unfortunately, all too often in business we try to circumvent the natural order of things by pushing forward without the proper internal alignment. Just as we plant seeds and watch their natural growth down and inwards, so we need to carefully plant the right structures for our organizational systems before trying to expand.

Yet, too often in corporations we push ourselves to move forward without the proper internal alignment. Interestingly, as companies become larger, their focus tends to shift inward. Customer relationships become less important and growth slows down. It turns out that most of the benefits of size are not positive. Why? Because we confuse growth with bigness. Bigness, unlike growth, is ultimately not sustainable. Growth on the other hand comes from developing resources to their full potential. This is harder to pull off than *expansion* but it is what real growth requires. People are your number one asset. No longer viewed as expenses, they need to be encouraged and inspired to achieve their full potential. More than any other activity, the development of people is at the heart of business growth.

When it comes to retention strategies, most companies think of salary increases, beefed-up benefits and more flexible schedules. However, business leaders are increasingly turning to coaching as another method to retain employees. Research indicates that companies know developing their employees is a very important activity. Many firms have realized that individuals value continuing education opportunities that empower them. It's a win-win scenario — both the individual and the company benefit. Coaching creates an environment of trust and alignment that accelerates the development of others so they can more effectively contribute to organizational goals.

It's Spring ... time to start planting those seeds. If you support and encourage the growth of your people now, your future harvest is guaranteed.

> *In everyone's life, at some time, our inner fire goes out. It is then burst into flame by an encounter with another human being. We should all be thankful for those people who rekindle the inner spirit.*
>
> — Albert Schweitzer

"Who are you?" is not a trick question!!! I was privileged to receive the Leadership Coaching of Phil Johnson, and looking back, I can't believe that once-upon-a-time I couldn't answer that question. I have to admit, the answer to that question is changing. As I continue to be myself I discover new things about myself, and remember some qualities of myself that I had almost forgotten. Phil's coaching came at a time when I was facing a serious family crisis. With humility, compassion, unconditional love and forgiveness — authentic leadership — I was able, as a parent to help my child and the rest of my family, survive a particularly difficult time. These days I express myself with qualities of humility and thankfulness. And as a thankful person, I am a richer person, perhaps because I take very little for granted. Phil, I am thankful for the help you have given me. Your book will inspire people to be themselves and in turn inspire others to do the same.

— Jean McNeil, Realtor

The Game Of
My Life!

I'd like to share with you the three distinct phases of my life, to illustrate how I was able to use my weaknesses as well as my strengths, to create a rewarding, new path for my career and personal life. If I can use a sports metaphor, the "game" of my life can be divided into the first half, half time, and second half.

FIRST HALF: 1953–1990

During the first half of my life, I took some vicious hits along the way. Diagnosed with dyslexia, I developed a strong, intuitive sense and became an over-achiever. The same energy that pushed me to succeed also caused me to rush through university, get married, start a family, embark on a career and climb continually upward, acquiring things along the way to make the journey more comfortable.

After scaling such a high peak, the valley that followed was one of divorce, guilt and loneliness. I had begun my journey with good intentions, but I suddenly found myself blindsided. Up until this point, I had not spent much time thinking about how I wanted to spend the rest of my life.

HALF TIME: 1990–2001

During "half time," I realized that keeping score of all my accomplishments did not offer the thrill it once did. Like Jack Nicholson's character in the famous movie, I wondered if this was "as good as it gets." I realized that I could not play the second half of my life the same way I had played the first, and I began to yearn for something more than material "success."

SECOND HALF: 2001–PRESENT

The second half of my life has brought a season of positive change. I fell in love, and I also rediscovered my passion: Leadership Coaching. The intuition I needed to develop as a child serves me well now as a Coach — there are no coincidences! I am now committed to giving back and leaving a legacy: making the rest of my life the best of my life. The eternity that seemed so far off in the first half is now within reach. I do not fear the end of the game but I would like to finish well and leave something behind.

> *You must be able to say no before you can truly say YES!*
> — Jeff Kennedy

Whether you are in first half, half time, or second half of your life, the clock is running but the game isn't over. You can make the rest of your life the best of your life. It's your choice — it always has been.

Make The Rest Of Your Life The Best Of Your Life

Working with Phil Johnson has helped me more than I would have imagined. It was refreshing to work with someone who did not have an agenda to change who I am. Rather, his objective was to understand who I am, what was important to me and why I was struggling in certain areas and ... by making some changes in how I was thinking and feeling that would allow me to address the things I was afraid of and the things I was struggling with.

— Jane Nelson,

VP Operations & Business Development

My Favorite Song

Row, row, row your boat,
Gently down the stream
Merrily, merrily, merrily, merrily,
Life is but a dream

It is time to speak your truth. Do not look outside yourself for the leader. We are the ones we've been waiting for.
— Oraibi, Arizona Hopi Nation

An eye-opening experience....

The Master of Business Leadership program has been an eye opening experience for me. Phil has gently helped me recognize my strengths and pointed out where I needed to concentrate in order to be a more effective leader. Through his techniques I discovered how I can be more effective in all my relationships both business and personal. He has an enthusiastic style that puts you at ease and allows you to open up. His coaching has helped me discover the authentic leader I really am.

Ron Percy
TEC Canada – Chair

The Puzzle Story

Picture this: It's a warm, Saturday morning during the summer, about 9AM, a beautiful day with not a cloud in the sky. Seven year-old Tommy is playing in the back-yard. He comes into the house, through the screen door, into the kitchen...through the kitchen... into the family room where he sees his dad sitting in his favourite chair... watching 10 or 15 things on TV.

Tommy runs up to his dad and hugs his leg: *Daddy, daddy you're home!*

Tommy's dad isn't home that much and he's excited to see him.

Can we go outside and play catch? Tommy asks.

His dad loves Tommy ... but he wants his "cave time" ... he needs his rest. So he says to Tommy, *Sure we can play catch, but before we play an outdoor game...let's play an indoor game...let's play a puzzle game.*

Tommy thinks this is great because he's playing with his dad and he loves his dad. So his dad searches around and he finds a map of the world tucked into a magazine. He and Tommy go into the dining room hand and hand. Tommy's dad begins to tear the map into lots of little pieces and spreads them out all over the table. Then he says, *OK, let's put the map of the world together...then we'll go outside and play catch.* Tommy thinks this is great. He pulls out a chair and kneels on it. Bending over the table, he begins to put the puzzle back together. As he becomes engrossed in the activity his dad skulks back into the family room and starts watching those 10 or 15 things on TV again.

About 20 minutes go by and Tommy comes running back into the family room and say, *Daddy, Daddy I'm done! Let's go outside and play catch!* His dad hears this and thinks to himself, *No way. It would have taken me at least 2 hours to put that puzzle together.* They go back into the dining room hand-in-hand and sure enough, the map of the world is sitting in the middle of the table. Tommy's dad starts laughing and says, *Tommy that's fantastic! How were you ever able to do it so quickly?* Tommy replies, *Well it was kind of hard in the beginning but I noticed on the back there was a picture of a little boy and when I put the little boy together the world came together.*

Be Your Piece Of The Puzzle And Inspire Others To Do The Same

When you're ill, you call the Doctor; when your teeth ache, you call the Dentist; when the plumbing is a problem, you call a Plumber; when you wake up one day and realize your life needs to take a new direction, you call Silicon Synergy and ask for Phil Johnson! Six months ago, sitting in a restaurant with Phil, turned out to be one of the very best things that could have happened to me. Perhaps even the best. Faced with a career change and feeling uncertain about myself and my future, I began working with Phil one day a week, identifying and carving out a path...a path moving in a preferable direction — forward. Phil, thanks to his

*outstanding coaching skills, character and rel-
ative experience, helped me navigate towards
my own business. He gave me the vision I needed
to get to where I am going. He taught me the
importance of action. It is the momentum. No
action, no results, no momentum. Made great
sense to me. From the moment we began this
journey, I felt safe. I felt I was not alone and I
felt there was always someone in my corner.
Much like an artist's brush stroke on a new
piece of canvas, each meeting with Phil added
more dimension and beauty to my life. I continue
to be a work in progress. I will continue to need
touch ups. Now, however, I have the vision and
the unique ability to add my own finishing
touches. Thank you Phil, very much.*

— Penny Dickenson, President

Do You Like Baseball?

An Extra Hit Goes A Long Way...

The difference between a player with a 333 batting average versus one with a 250 average may surprise you.

A 333 player is very important to his team's success. He may be the team's *franchise* player and may be earning over $30M per year. He's probably been with the team for several years having signed a long-term contract. He has TV commercials and a line of clothing named after him ... maybe even a book or movie.

A 250 player has probably been on several teams and has a one-year contract. He is a *utility* player that does not play every day. He may be making close to the league minimum salary ... he does not have a line of clothing named after him, and I doubt there will be a book or movie any time soon.

> *Be so good they can't ignore you.*
> — Steve Martin

Do you know what the difference is between these two players?

One hit, every three days.

In an average game, a player comes to bat 4 times. In 3 days he will bat 12 times. A 250 hitter will get three hits ... a 333-hitter gets four. That little extra effort can make an incredible difference. By taking action and making small changes you can experience dramatic results.

Just one extra hit, every three days!

Monkey Business:

How to Design a company Policy That Will Drive Your Employees Bananas!

Start with a cage containing five monkeys. Inside the cage, hang a banana on a string and place a set of stairs under it. Before long, a monkey will go to the stairs and start to climb towards the banana.

As soon as the monkey touches the stairs, spray all the other monkeys with cold water. After a while, another monkey will make an attempt. Spray all the other monkeys with cold water again. Pretty soon, when another monkey tries to climb the stairs the other monkeys will try to prevent it.

Now, put the water away. Remove one monkey from the cage and replace it with a new one. The new monkey will see the banana and want to climb the stairs. To his surprise and horror, all of the other monkeys will attack him. After another attempt and attack, he will know that if he tries to climb the stairs he will be assaulted.

Next, remove another of the original five monkeys and replace it with a new one. The newcomer will go to the stairs and be attacked by the other monkeys. The previous newcomer will take part in the punishment with enthusiasm! Likewise, replace the third original monkey with a new one, then a fourth, then the fifth.

Every time the newest monkey takes to the stairs, he will be attacked. Most of the monkeys that are beating him will have no idea why they are not permitted to climb the stairs or why they are participating in the beating of the newest monkey.

After replacing all of the original monkeys, none of the remaining monkeys have ever been sprayed with cold water. Nevertheless, no monkey ever again approaches the stairs to try for the banana.

Why not? Because as far as they know, that's the way it's always been done around here.

If you always do what you've always done, you'll always get what you always got. — Wizard Of Oz

During my second or third coaching session, Phil said that I was a "good student", which is hilarious because I've always thought of myself as a terrible student. In fact, most of the time I suffer from attention deficit disorder. So for me, sitting through the thirteen-week program and really listening was a stretch. But I did it, and I think I did a pretty good job to boot. Maybe it's because my disposition was already there and open in terms of some of the leadership concepts Phil was relaying, but mostly because it was simple and made sense.

Phil's concepts were like drinking a fresh, cold glass of water. They went down smoothly and totally refreshed me, or rather, my perspective on people. His philosophy is that for us to expect the best in our people, it starts with "you" being who you are. How true is that? How on earth can I

*expect my salespeople to be more passionate /
creative / enthusiastic / customer friendly /
value centric / etc, if I myself am not being a
leader in those areas? I see it everyday, when I
get passionate about an opportunity to help a
client, it sparks the fires of enthusiasm in my
people. Being who you truly are and inspiring
others — what a wonderful truth.*

*There are so many powerful concepts that
Phil has helped me grasp, or rather, solidify. He
helped me to put a framework around
leadership and moreover, understand the
impact of both negative and positive behaviors
on others. I am certain you will enjoy reading
this book and interacting with him through
the MBL Coaching Program as much as I
did. His concepts have already helped us close
$500,000 in business with much more in the
pipe! How's that for quantifiable value and
ROI.*

— Joanne Moretti, GM & SVP

Leaders And Victims

Victims make mistakes and say, "I'm sorry," but do the same thing the next time.

Leaders make mistakes and say, "I made a mistake," and make up for it.

Victims say, "I'm not as bad as a lot of other people."

Leaders say, "I'm good, but not as good as I can be yet."

Victims get compliments and make excuses or jokes.

Leaders get compliments and say, "Thank you."

Victims are affected by others.

Leaders affect others.

Victims would rather be liked than admired, and wind up having little of either.

Leaders would rather be admired than liked, and wind up having an abundance of both.

Victims resent others and try to find their faults.

Leaders respect others and try to learn something from them.

Victims stand FOR nothing and fight against everything — even themselves.

Leaders stand FOR something and are willing to fight FOR it if necessary.

Do You Know What You Don't Know?

Being smart is no longer enough if you want to succeed in business. There is a crucial difference between the appearance of leadership and the actual ability to run a 21st Century enterprise. Business success depends upon the development of leaders with wisdom. Being highly intelligent does not mean a person is wise. Many business leaders today are intelligent but not all of them are wise. To earn this distinction, their most important ability is acknowledging what they don't know.

Metacognition is the ability to know whether you know. If you know what to you don't know, you are less likely to make bad decisions based on misplaced confidence in your own intelligence. If you are aware of your ignorance you can educate yourself. Leaders with poor metacognition never understand that they don't understand, nor do they know what's missing. That's not wise.

Even young children will admit when they don't know the answer. Their young minds have not been confused by too much information or clouded with ego.

There is so much to know in the world that even the most brilliant minds only grasp the tiniest fraction. Thus, we should always be in doubt of what we think we know.

**Want more expertise or a coaching session?
Contact Phil Johnson:**

Phil Johnson, MBL Coach

Silicon Synergy Inc

Bus: 905-272-5690

Cell: 416-729-7445

MBLCoach@MasterofBusinessLeadership.com

MasterofBusinessLeadership.com

MasterofBusinessLeadership.blogspot.com

Authentic
Leadership

Workforce Engagement

I'll Give You Wood When You Give Me Heat

According to a survey by Badbossology.com a majority of employees spend ten or more hours per month complaining or listening to others complain about bad bosses — and almost one-third spend twenty hours or more per month.

While the survey is intended to point out why bosses need to be coached so they can become better leaders, the results also point out why employees need to be coached so they can change their behaviour. There are several reasons why they should not engage in counter-productive boss bashing, even if they do have a bad boss.

The downside of "boss bashing":

- Wastes Time
- Demeans Yourself
- Hurts Your Company
- Communicates A Lack Of Courage
- Depresses Yourself And Others
- Does Not Enhance Your Career

When you seek to control another and the other person lets you, who is preying upon whom? Victims prey upon each other.

PRINCIPALS IN ACTION

Janine, one of my clients, was struggling with an abrasive colleague and becoming increasingly upset as hostility and tension escalated between the two of them. I reminded her that sometimes we need to be willing to give *more*, even when we feel justified in giving less. Keeping this principle in mind, Janine reported a "miracle" during our next session. Her colleague had phoned her that very afternoon, yelling and upset that she had interfered in a matter belonging to his department. In the past, she admits she would have yelled back, convinced of the need to defend herself from his verbal onslaught. However, she now concedes this would only have caused further deterioration of their relationship. This time, she simply said, "I'm sorry," to which she received stunned silence on the other end of the line. Janine continued, "You're absolutely right, I should have come to you about this issue. I totally respect your position as head of your department." Taken aback, her colleague stammered, "I'm sorry — I'm yelling. I'm just upset. It's been a terrible day." My client replied, "That's ok, I understand. What can I do to help you?"

Now, Janine's colleague was floored! This two minute exchange became an important turning point in their work relationship which slowly began to thaw over time, all because Janine was willing to give *more*, instead of less.

TAKE ACTION!

In what areas of your life are you holding back? How could you become more fully engaged? What work relationship conflicts could benefit by you giving *wood*, instead of waiting for the other person to give you *heat*?

> Make a list of three concrete actions you can take, and implement them this week.

Life — It's Not Long Enough!

Throughout history, truly authentic leaders have continued to inspire others long after their deaths. The legacy of their life's work may actually have taken on more significance for us as we have grown and developed. Leaders of the past have left us incredible messages because they wanted to connect with and serve not only current, but also future generations. They knew their lives would not be long enough.

The global economy has shown us that our lives and actions are all interconnected: past, present and future. Regardless of how long you live the only real question is, *What are you going to do with the time you have left?*

> We Are Evolving From The View And
> Pursuit Of Power As External To The
> Pursuit Of Authentic Power
> It's All About Being Who You Are

TAKE ACTION!

What legacy would you like to leave behind, for your family, friends and others? Imagine that you are present at your own funeral. What sorts of things would you like people to say about you? What would you like your tombstone to read? Make a list of the five most important goals you will accomplish: this year, in five years, in ten years, and by the end of your life. Now, make a list of three concrete things you can do to get started on your goals, beginning today.

Intuition And Consciousness

Our intuition is developed as we connect with our internal power. We have evolved as far as intellect will take us. As a species, we are moving from the view and pursuit of power and leadership as external to the pursuit of authentic internal power. Changing our unconscious perceptions, habits and beliefs will change our results. The connection to the universal intelligence is through our unconscious mind.

Einstein came up with the Theory of Relativity while daydreaming - something he did frequently (as dyslexics are prone to do). Because it was something he did not conclude rationally, he had a difficult time believing it could be true. And some people feel his contributions to the world stalled after that "discovery" because he was obsessed with trying to disprove his theory.

One of the things has always interested me about this story was that he frequently stopped on purpose to "daydream" (which associates with our "Alpha Theta and Delta" brain waves). He was actually taking a break to meditate. His regular meditations were going ever deeper, where he was achieving the slower brain waves that indicate heightened intuition or creativity and a more expansive mental state. This was how he came up with the Theory of Relativity. You might say rationalism (or logic alone - Beta Waves) killed Einstein's creativity. Words like intuition, meditation and creativity are the lay meanings those sensations can be linked to measurable brain waves. Meditation, completely natural (like sleep), takes you neurologically through the same steps as sleeping, but in a conscious state. Just like sleep, meditation will take your brain through the different waves. The more you meditate, the easier it gets, and the deeper it gets. You also get better at distinguishing the depth of your meditations. Like

Einstein I was also born with dyslexia. When I have exhausted my conscious mind I frequently stop and meditate. Most of the time, new unexpected ideas are attracted to me.

Authentic leaders see both the reality and the illusion - victims see only he illusion.

We've Entered A Period Of Rapid Evolution

We are awakening to the reality that almost every-thing we thought we knew is an illusion. Our search for external power and leadership has created the fear and disengagement that sets individuals and corporations against each other. All of our social, economic and political institutions reflect this understanding of power and leadership as external.

But we are evolving rapidly into an awareness of our authentic internal power and leadership. Companies and individuals are becoming more consciously engaged in this journey. We live in a feelings economy.

The concept of emotional intelligence has taken center stage. Organizations have typically hired for IQ and fired for a lack of EQ. The essential difference: Emotion leads to action while reason leads to conclusions. Reason is not a motivator. It is clear that people are more engaged by compassion than truth, although both are essential.

Authentic feelings and actions inspire the highest levels of workforce engagement. The feeling your product or service creates is the true wealth that is reflected in your results.

Authentic
Leadership

There is great irony in the fact that personal ambitions driving people to positions of power are at odds with the humility required for authentic leadership. Boards of directors frequently believe they need to hire larger-than-life, egocentric leaders to make their organizations great. In these types of organizations, leaders are measured by the degree to which they have mastered the external environment and delivered results in the form of revenues, profits, new product breakthroughs, cost savings, or market share increases.

But leadership is not simply something we do. It comes from somewhere inside us. Leadership is a process, an expression of who we are. At its deepest level, *leadership is authentic self-expression that creates value.* I like to refer to this as YDV x Q ... Your Distinctive

Value times the Quantity of people affected. It is a blend of personal humility and professional will. Leadership begins and ends with authenticity. It is being yourself — being the person you were created to be. This is not what most of the literature on leadership says, nor is it what the "experts" teach. Instead, they develop lists of leadership characteristics that one is supposed to emulate. They describe the styles of leaders and suggest that you adopt them, rather than encouraging you to develop *yourself*.

The goal of all truly authentic leaders is to inspire each of us to develop our own unique abilities. During the 1990s, there was a media campaign with the following slogan — *I Want To Be Like Mike*. This type of message only serves to hinder leadership development. Think about it: if Michael Jordan had wanted to be like anyone other than himself, he would not have been able to generate the results he achieved.

Trying to be like someone else is the opposite of authenticity. Unfortunately, the media, the business press, and even the movies, glorify leaders with high-ego personalities. They focus on the style of leaders, not their character. In large measure, making heroes out of celebrity CEOs is at the heart of the crisis in corporate leadership.

Authentic leadership is not about changing who you are — *it's about being who you are*. It's not hard but it isn't easy.

Integrity is the alignment of what you think, say and do. This definition applies equally to both individuals and corporations. — Phil Johnson

While on business in China, Randall took time to reflect upon his Master of Business Leadership experience: Phil is my buddy — my mentor — a father figure — that wise old man on top of the hill (and he has the grey hairs to match!) Each session of Phil's MBL course was a mini-epiphany for me: yes, the win/lose model is old school; yes, there is plenty to go around; yes, somebody else loves the work you consider boring; yes, a leader is measured by his respect and not by the volume of his voice. These were intangible truths I knew to be real but couldn't find in the business world... Phil broke down what it means to be an Authentic Leader and gave me the tools to communicate these values to my team. I am now more myself, more of a leader, more effective, and more happy in my work... and personal life. Phil, I thank you for showing me the road and staying with me throughout the journey — I look forward to our friendship, lessons, and laughter in the years to come.

— Randall Mileski,
Senior System Design Engineer

Invisible
Leadership

A true leader is frequently a low profile person who understands the vital importance of staying on top of trends and developments, taking small, almost invisible action on issues before they grow into problems. Such leaders are the unsung heroes who are building the organization's future one small brick at a time.

In many organizations today, we are encouraged to do great things. We believe this means that we need substantial problems to solve, so we'll often wait until the issue has become a problem before we act. There is little glory in resolving small issues, much more in saving the day in the face of catastrophe. Our focus and horizons are too short. We are making headway for the moment but there may be insurmountable problems yet to come. Are we winning the battle and losing the war? True leaders know that it doesn't take a cataclysm to destroy an organization, just the accumulated erosion of small, apparently inconsequential events, so readily passed over by the battle heroes. We, who applaud the spectacular achievements of today's corporate warriors, need to remember that it is the meek who shall inherit the earth.

The "S" Word: Spirituality

CEOs and managers need to lead with integrity and passion. Their spiritual quotient (SQ) is at the heart of authentic leadership. A "boss" in touch with his inner self will do a better job. Today's leader must be authentic, inspire, nurture and lead with high ethical standards.

Good leaders have the ability to arouse "discretionary energy" in others. Their passion inspires a higher level of contribution by those around them. As a Servant-Warrior, a leader is more compassionate, insightful and facilitative in his or her business and personal relationships.

The combination of IQ with EQ and SQ leads to better decisions, greater resource alignment, faster time-to-market and ultimately better bottom-line results. Spirituality is an emerging mega-trend and is surprisingly practical in business. Its absence can lead to arrogance and greed.

Employees are longing for leaders they can trust, underscoring the need for authentic leadership infused with spirituality.

> *Tell me what you're for — not what you're against.*
>
> — Phil Johnson

Conflict And Consensus Decisions

Business leaders need to actively create and encourage a culture that allows for the expression of opposing viewpoints on the way to reaching consensus decisions. A "consensus decision" is a decision that everyone can and will live with. By advocating the expression of dissenting viewpoints, you can create a climate where ethical wrongdoing will not go unchallenged. It is important to invite dissent and debate within the decision-making group. Individual status and position-based power needs to be eliminated during group discussions. You may want to employ devil's advocates as you search for and test multiple possibilities as solutions.

It is important to treat each other with trust and

respect while working to keep the conflict constructive. There is great value to be found inside corporate diversity, and this can be a key strength in corporate decision-making. When people within an organization are in consensus, their various tasks and activities automatically operate in alignment. Faster time-to-market and better resource utilization are just a few of the potential benefits.

Authentic leaders can facilitate this type of conflict-consensus process so that synergistic results are achieved and no one gets left behind.

REFLECT

When was the last time your company needed to make an important decision? How was the decision made, what process was used? Was it a consensus decision? If not, how did others react to it? Have you noticed any negative consequences as a result of using a "top-down" decision making process?

Leaders inspire people to feel that they are at the very heart of things, not on the periphery. Everyone feels they make a difference to the success of the organization.
— Warren Bennis

How might implementing a consensus decision-making process produce better results next time?

> *Working with Phil has been a truly enlightening experience. His common sense approach to leadership has not only helped me look within myself but also helped me in recognizing the leaders around me! It truly is not about everyone else but about me and my life. This has changed the way I approach every difficult situation and the way that I live my life. I am so much more aware of what I do, how I react and how every situation makes me feel. There is no more excuse that I do not know what to do. I WILL NOT BE THE VICTIM! I AM THE LEADER!!*
>
> — Amandio Pereira, VP Sales Enablement

Sales
Leadership

In 1964, the Harvard Business Review published an article entitled, "What Makes A Good Salesman." After seven years of field research, the authors concluded the two qualities all successful salespeople had in common were empathy and ego drive.

They were only half right.

True sales leadership requires empathy and courage — not ego. Ego is a fear-based response to win-lose relationships where the focus is on *conquest* and *getting the sale*. The true sales professional understands that generating revenue is not their *primary objective* — it is the *result* of developing relationships, solving problems and aligning resources. This awareness serves to focus their activities and strengthens the relationship.

The real value in a business relationship is the relationship itself. When you add your company's resources in a way that increases theirs, you create value for them. When you use your abilities to solve a problem for someone or enable them to capture an opportunity, you earn a level of trust and respect, which deepens the relationship. This allows you to create even more value as you engage with the individual on a personal level. Their appreciation combined with a focus on creating value results in a strong, enduring relationship.

So why is it important for sales professionals to be leaders?

The reason is that building relationships, solving problems and aligning company resources requires *risk*. Taking action requires both trust and a willingness to take risk. Risk is involved because many times we cannot see the end result without first taking the action. The seeing comes after the action has been taken. Taking action requires us to acknowledge and move through our fears. The stories that we tell ourselves may be coloring our views. When action is taken the stories that we tell ourselves begin to change.

The courage to take positive action and lead the way ultimately comes from self-knowledge. We are all selling something — a product, a service — an idea. Global opportunities abound but they are not for the faint of heart. Could you or your sales team use a little more courage?

> *Seriousness is a disease that can be cured.* — Ross Quinn

When I first sat down with Phil, I thought it would be a run of the mill session on how to be a better person. I thought it would focus on how I can listen better or be clearer on what I say so that those around me would be better off for the time spent. The desired result was the same but the journey was a much different one and much more exciting. To look within yourself and understand that you are one unique piece that is interdependent on the entire puzzle functioning together is a sobering realization. Phil allowed me to take stock of my life and live in the moment. The Master of Business Leadership enabled me to focus on me, which is a nice change with this thing called Life happening all around us. I can only dream of being an inspiration to others and feel that I am at the start of my journey, thanks to Phil, of realizing my vision statement.

— Alan MacDonald, GSO

Closing The Solution-Value Gap

Is your company being paid for the value of its products or services?

Customers and clients know when they have a problem that can be solved by others' resources, but it may not be entirely understood by them.

Your customer may even be using external consultants to help them better understand the problem. As solution providers, we often make the mistaken assumption that our customers fully understand their problems and we focus on potential solutions. In reality, the solution-decision process may be delayed or even abandoned entirely without a complete understanding of the problem to be solved. This problem-solution value gap may cause your company to feel pressured into stripping value out of the solution as a result of downward pricing pressures.

As a *Solution Sales Leader* you can deepen your business relationships and credibility by working to close this gap. Any potential solution can only be fully appreciated when the problem and its associated costs to the organization are completely understood.

Closing The Solution-Value Gap:

In order to close the solution-value gap, ask yourself the following:

1. What are the customer's business objectives?
2. What are their critical success factors?
3. What is the problem in the absence of your solution?
4. What are the causes of the problem?
5. What are the costs and consequences of the problem to the organization?
6. What are the desired outcomes expected as a result of using your solution?

By leading your customer through this solution-value process you can close the gap and turn a soft skill into hard results.

Business Leadership MOJO — Know who you are, what you want out of the business and why.
— Bo Burlingham

Obtaining my MBL was an excellent experience — thanks a lot Phil for your help and guidance! It's amazing how some basic principles can so dramatically change the way you look at different situations and ultimately your life. Phil is a terrific coach and I strongly encourage anyone and everyone to take this program because "you don't know what you don't know".
— Raj Juneja, Sales Manager

When I started my Leadership coaching with Phil, I knew it would be a challenge because I would have to face my fears to get through this experience successfully. In order to evolve as a Leader you must move beyond your fears, habits and perceptions. I now understand through my coaching, that you need to take action and the Leader in you emerges and you become a better person. I also know that we are never done growing as individuals. It was a great experience for me!

— Renee Lalonde, VP Sales

Emotional Intelligence

IQ and technical skills are important, but emotional intelligence is the sine qua non (without which it could not be) of authentic leadership.

When asked to define the ideal leader, many would emphasize traits such as intelligence, toughness, determination, and vision - the qualities traditionally associated with leadership. Such skills are necessary but insufficient qualities for the leader. Although a certain degree of analytical and technical skill is a minimum requirement for success, studies indicate that emotional intelligence may be the key attribute that distinguishes outstanding performers from those who are merely adequate.

Psychologist and author Daniel Goleman first brought the term "emotional intelligence" to a wide audience with his 1995 book of the same name. In his research at nearly 200 large, global companies, Goleman found that truly effective leaders are distinguished by a high degree of emotional intelligence. Without it, a person can have first-class training, an incisive mind, and an endless supply of good ideas, but he still won't be a great leader. Both Goleman, cochair of the Consortium for Research on Emotional Intelligence in Organizations, based at Rutgers University and Phil Johnson, Master of Business Leadership Coach have found direct ties between emotional intelligence and measurable business results.

Stop Marketing To Strangers

REFERRALS: YOUR UNTAPPED RESERVOIR OF OPPORTUNITY

Your company may be spending up to one third of its time and money marketing to relative strangers while ignoring existing clients and customers.

Within your base of customers there is a core of strong business relationships. The 20 people or companies that make up 80 percent of your revenue are already using your product or service. They have a warm market of at least 20 people or companies just like them. And those people also have a warm market of 20 people or companies. This represents eight thousand (8,000) warm market prospects within two degrees of separation from you and your business — a very large reservoir of untapped opportunity.

As business leaders, we need to have the courage to risk focusing more of our resources on this group. Whether you want more customers or not, you can benefit immediately from deepening your connection with the ones you already have. They will introduce you to other people like them if they feel you are creating value for them and they like the experience of dealing with your company.

When you deliver a quality product or service, you create a niche for your organization. The smaller the niche, the bigger the market. At this point the market becomes the marketer. When you are focused on doing your best for others they will do their best to refer and promote your business to people you might never have reached — literally multiplying your opportunities. You might even consider using part of your existing marketing budget to promote this type of customer and client networking activity.

Are We Paying You Enough?

You heard right.

Do any of your clients or customers ever ask you if they are paying you enough for your product or service? If not, it may be an indication that your business relationships could be better.

The most efficient use of available resources, the fastest time-to-market and the greatest profitability occur when your company's success and your client's success become interdependent. As time passes, you come to realize that your mutual business relationship has become a critically important component of your organization's ultimate success.

Business relationships are living things that deepen as greater value is created. Interdependent cooperation and synergistic results are created. Companies need strong business relationships.

Are your clients asking you this question?

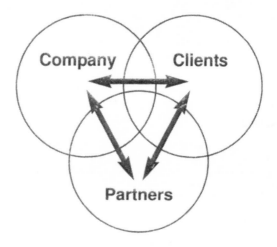

Environmental Survey

As part of this exercise I would like you to become an objective observer of your environment for the next 24 hours. Simply observe and record the activities you encounter during this period. They might include reading a newspaper, watching a TV program, video games, conversations, books, food, shopping, work, music, radio programs, relationships, magazines, entertainment, travel, leisure, sports, the news, education, family, friends, co-workers, business partners, exercise, meetings, etc.

Was the activity you observed predominantly *Win/Win or Win/Lose?

WIN/WIN	WIN/LOSE
_____	_____
_____	_____
_____	_____
_____	_____
_____	_____

*Win/Win — All Participants, On All Sides Win At The Same Time

Love Is The Killer App

Tim Sanders, Yahoo
Chief Solutions Officer

Faith beats fear, greed isn't good and
nice guys finish first. Really.

The most powerful force in business is love. It's what will
help your company grow and become stronger. It's what will
propel your career forward. It's what will give you a sense of
meaning and satisfaction in your work, which will help you
do your best work. — Tim Sanders, Yahoo Chief Solutions
Officer

> There Is Only
> Love & Fear —
> And Fear Is
> Irrelevant
> — Phil Johnson

Love isn't a business concept — it's a way of life. Compassion and empathy aren't management tools to be pulled out when needed. They're character traits that true leaders possess. If people are your most important asset and customers are king — these slogans must be reflected in your actions.

Synergy And Team Work

Synergy is about creative cooperation and teamwork. It results from valuing differences and bring- ing different perspectives together in the spirit of mutual trust and respect. Synergy is the phenomenon that occurs when people working together perform and achieve far beyond what they could accomplish separately. It is a cooperative effort that yields a combined effect.

When synergy is lacking, people are not working effi- ciently and effectively towards shared goals. They may be more focused on achieving personal agendas than on reaching team objectives. Energy and creativity may be wasted in non-productive friction with people who are "unengaged" for various reasons. At times, it can feel like an engine with spark plugs firing at the wrong time, wasting energy that could be used to propel the vehicle forward.

Synergy provides motivational and creative energy. It is a catalyst that helps people harmonize and grow together to produce desired results. Productivity increases and stress is reduced as individuals contribute their respective strengths towards a common goal.

Authentic leaders have the ability to inspire higher levels of synergy and engagement within their organizations.

REFLECT

- What are you doing to create synergy within your organization?
- Who should you have synergy with? Why?

Authentic Leadership — It's Good For Your Health

Developing authentic leadership is not only good for your business — it's good for your health.

From at least as far back as Aristotle, the need for balance has been recognized as a way of avoiding *disease*. Illness was thought to arise from being out of balance. The same can be said about dysfunctional organizations. Healthy businesses exhibit a balance of ethics, enthusiasm, evaluation and empathy. These are also traits seen in authentic leaders.

Each individual needs to develop his or her own leadership style.

Authentic leaders lead with purpose, meaning, and values. They build enduring relationships with people. They are consistent and self-disciplined. When their principles are tested, they refuse to compromise. Authentic leaders and organisations are dedicated to developing themselves and they seek to serve as they inspire others.

Leadership
And Coaching

Authentic Leadership Is Wealth

You can have wealth without money. If you had a machine that made anything you wanted, you wouldn't need money. Wealth is what we want - money is a way of moving wealth. In practice they are usually interchangeable but they are not the same. There's a fixed amount of money but not a fixed amount of wealth. We can make more wealth. Kids without money create wealth by making gifts. Employees work together to create wealth.

The current level of workforce engagement at creating wealth is a mere 29 percent. Employees have lost their interest in working together to create wealth. Position-based power "leadership" that many businesses use has created victims and low levels of workforce engagement. The development of Authentic Leadership is THE SOLUTION.

Authentic leadership creates personal wealth and inspires synergistic organizational wealth creation within the company. More than 75 per cent of wealth created today is service related. The intangible capital (patents, R&D, services, etc.) of the world's largest 150 companies has been estimated at $7.5 trillion - up from $800 billion just a decade ago. Authentic leadership is wealth - it's what people want and companies need.

The Results Habit

As business leaders we need to be clear in our communications. Each one of us needs to understand, agree and be personally committed to what we are responsible for delivering. Stay focused on the most important objectives. In order to accomplish this we will need to become experts at saying "no." Things which matter most must never be at the mercy of things which matter least — *Johann Goethe*. And the things that matter most must get done.

These desired results must be clear and measurable. Con-

> Realize that at the beginning of the day, it's all about possibilities. At the end of the day it's all about results. — Bob Prosen

versations need to be action oriented (What did you do? What did you learn? How did you feel? What's next?). Finally, rewards need to be linked to the targeted results.

Leadership
And Success
Coaching
An Emerging Industry

THE BENEFITS OF COACHING
SURVEY

Leadership and success coaching is an emerging industry. A recent survey on executive coaching conducted
by The Institute of Executive Development (Palo Alto,
CA February 2006) indicated that its popularity in the last
few years is only the beginning of continued growth for
the field, and many organizations are expecting to

spend more on coaching in the next few years. The survey examined responses from over 200 organizations from 12 different industry sectors. The survey found that while coaching is conducted in a relatively small percentage of organizations, those who have started programs use coaching for multiple layers of management, and plan to spend quite aggressively in the future.

Few organizations have formal coaching. Sixty one percent of respondents said they have either limited, or no coaching in their organizations today. Additionally, the vast majority (70%) have started a formal program only within the last three years, with 43% having no formal program currently. However, spending is poised to accelerate. Organizational spending on coaching has remained stable or grown for the vast majority of respondents over the past three years. Amazingly, almost half of all respondents forecast growth of over 10% per year over the next three years.

This information points toward executive coaching, as an industry, taking on a different shape in the years to come. Coaching will experience a dramatic evolution over the next few years — from an activity-based exercise to a results-focused experience. In terms of costs, the majority report per participant costs of over $10,000, and 30% report per participant costs of over $20,000. Interestingly, many organizations have not yet fully integrated coaching into other developmental programs that they offer.

"Nothing is more powerful than an idea whose time has come." - Victor Hugo

The challenge of being who you are is both simple and complex at the same time. With Phil's MBL coaching I have been afforded a framework that is helping me work through my fears, habits and perceptions and those of my team members, associates, family and friends, to inspire them to be who they are. He is right, after completing the three-month program, I have lost the excuse that I do not know what to do next...thank you Phil!

— Steve Koslowski, Regional Manager

**Want more expertise or a coaching session?
Contact Phil Johnson:**

Phil Johnson, MBL Coach

Silicon Synergy Inc

Bus: 905-272-5690

Cell: 416-729-7445

MBLCoach@MasterofBusinessLeadership.com

MasterofBusinessLeadership.com

MasterofBusinessLeadership.blogspot.com

Master of Business Leadership

COACHING QUESTIONNAIRE

The following are some examples of the questions we ask our MBL coaching clients at the beginning of the program. You may want to reflect upon and answer them for yourself. By taking action, you can change the stories you tell yourself that currently prevent you from reaching your goals.

- Do you love what you do?
- Do you consider yourself to be a success?
- What's the one thing you want to do better?

- Close your eyes and take a few deep breathes. Now imagine that you are 95 years old and about to take your last breathe. If you could go back in time to today, to this very moment — what advice would you give the person you are at this moment?
- What professional advice would the 95 year old have for you?
- What personal advice would the 95 year old have?
- What are your unique abilities?
- What gives you energy and engages your passion?
- Who are you?
- What do you want long term, for your career? Please be specific.
- How good are you at accepting help from others?
- How can you make the most difference with the least effort?
- What would you consider to be the *Defining Moment* in your life and in your career to this point?
- Have you ever played a win-win game (where everyone wins at the same time)?

- What is the one thing that you should stop doing and the one thing that you should start doing?
- In what areas of your personal life are you holding back?
- In what areas of your business life are you holding back?
- What would your family, friends and colleagues say are the driving forces in your life?
- What would you say are the driving forces in your life?
- How can you make the best use of your talents?
- How important is *free time* to you?
- What are the most powerful ways you can increase your value to others?
- What's keeping you from being who you are?
- Would you like to retire some day? Why? What would you do differently?
- How do you have fun?
- How could you develop more self-confidence?
- What is the real value of a business relationship?
- What is the most important thing you and I should

be talking about during this coaching process?

- How is this issue impacting you? What else is being impacted?
- What is the most important step you can take to begin to resolve this issue?
- What are your biggest frustrations at this moment?
- Is there any one activity that, if you did it extremely well, would produce outstanding results?
- What would you need to see and feel to become more "engaged" in your current role?
- What do you want your legacy to be?
- If you were your own Coach, what suggestions would you have for yourself?
- Describe what your perfect life would look like.
- Take a few minutes to consider the end of your life. How do you want people to remember you?

Habits

We are all committed to our current habits. What's more, we developed these habits as a successful response to various stressful situations. We continued to use and refine them because they got us the results we wanted at one point in our lives. But what worked for us then may be killing us now. So, how does a person or company change a thinking pattern that no longer serves them? You make a choice to do something different. By taking different actions, you get different results and you develop new habits. As this occurs the "story" you tell yourself will change.

Any time you experience frustration with these new actions, realize that it is being caused by your old programming trying to push you back into old behaviours. This programming is buried in your subconscious mind and it drives your behaviour on a daily basis. The mark of a Master is the person who has the ability to give him or herself a command and then follow it! These programs or paradigms came from outside sources and we often accepted them without question. Many times our paradigm contains lack and limitation because a parent, teacher, coach or another person we respected wanted to protect us from disappointment. They told us to "be realistic," "don't expect too much," "life is hard" and many other disempowering beliefs. The moment you accept their programs, they drive your behaviour and often limit your results.

The Courage Individuals And Companies Exhibit While Beginning To Act Differently Produces Greater Confidence And Is Ultimately The True Measure Of The Importance Of The Desired Result

Stages of Growth
And Experience
Time-Spaced Learning

6. Celebration

1. Action

5. Illumination

2. Confusion

4. Incubation

3. Exploration

Change Happens Instantly — Getting To That
Point Can Take Time

*Action > Leader/Victim Awareness/Choice >
Individual And Organizational Healing*

Individual And Synergistic Group Results		
Unconscious Incompetent	**Bliss ...**	Connectedness, innocence, focus internal, receivers, positive energy
Phase I (Individual Choice)		
Conscious Incompetent		Struggle and conflict in the search for position based external power. The ego is created, focus external, achievers, takers, control, scarcity mentality, negative energy.
Phase II (Awareness)		
Conscious Competent		Awareness and confusion — necessary for integration and growth.
Phase III (Interconnectedness)		
Unconscious Competent	**Mastery ...**	Interconnectedness, intuition, wisdom, grace, calm, internal power, courageous, reverent, respectful, abundance mentality, high positive energy.

STAGES OF GROWTH AND EXPERIENCE

STAGE I

Unconscious Incompetence

During the first stage of growth, we are unconscious that we are incompetent. We experience this stage as one of connectedness and innocence. Our focus is internal, we are willing receivers, and we exude positive energy. This is the "bliss" stage, where our ignorance of our own incompetence keeps us happily unaware of our need to grow.

Case Illustration: "Sydney" is a new editor for a magazine publication. She enthusiastically hires friend after friend to provide her with articles, despite their lack of experience and professionalism. She feels happy and positive in her job, and is unaware of her colleagues' frustration that the work being handed in late by her writers is causing delays in production.

STAGE II

Conscious Incompetence

This stage is characterized by awareness of your problem, as well as confusion about how to solve it. Stage II is necessary for integration and growth.

Case Illustration: Sydney realizes that she has a problem: articles being handed in late by her friends have delayed production to the point that her Creative Director has angrily resigned, calling her "incompetent" and "unprofessional." She realizes that she will have to take action, but is unsure how to achieve her goal of a smoothly running editorial department.

STAGE III

Conscious Competence

Sydney gradually learns that to do her job well, she must hire only professional writers and develop a system of checks and balances to ensure that editorial is handed in on time.

STAGE IV

Mastery

This stage is the other side of the coin from "bliss." In this stage, you feel connected; you have clarity, intuition, wisdom, grace, calm and inner focus.

Case Illustration: Sydney is now completely adept at running her department. Editorial flows through a well-regulated system on time, and she is able to complete her work with calmness and ease.

That old saying holds true for me, when the student is ready the Master appears. That was my exact experience with seeking Phil's services as a Coach. I knew when I met Phil that he had something to teach me and I was totally correct. Phil assisted me to realize that Leadership is a choice each and every day and the only time that really exists is "now". He helped me get reconnected to my internal Leadership and to actively be that and thereby I was able to find happiness right now versus waiting for it to "happen". Happiness is also a choice and I have decided, with Phil's coaching, that I want that right now versus at some elusive time in the future. I will be forever grateful for Phil's coaching.

— Jane Zorn, Director

The Looming Talent Retention And Engagement Challenge

A Deloitte research report suggests that globalization in 2008 is proving to be a contest for resources, both natural and human. There is an acute shortage of talent and workforce engagement. In an age in which growth is largely a product of both creative and technological advances, companies must be able to attract and retain talented employees. They must also engage people like never before if they want to innovate and grow. Only those companies that win the hearts and minds of their employees will be able to deliver value over both the short and long terms.

Responding to today's workplace demands means that firms must offer more than a good paycheque. Record-high numbers of disaffected workers already cost organizations millions of dollars in lost productivity. In the face of such challenges, traditional approaches to managing talent fall short. A more thoughtful response is required - one that engages employees in ways that promote the flexibility and productivity needed to compete.

Waves of downsizing, employer demands, job disenchantment and technologies that keep employees plugged into their jobs both day and night have taken their toll. If recent surveys are an indication, more than half the workforce is fed up. Emerging research suggests that workforce toxicity is the number one factor when it comes to employee morale and performance.

Annual Cost Of Employee Disenchantment
Gallup Semi-Annual Employee Engagement Index

29% Are Actively Engaged In Their Jobs

54% Are Not-Engaged

17% Are Actively Disengaged

- France 100 Billion Euros
- UK $64 Billion
- Singapore $6 Billion
- United States $350 Billion

Organizations may want to first examine the development of their people rather than technology-based solutions. The evidence is undeniable, the position-based power and management model has and will continue to produce poor results. Greater levels of engagement and results can be achieved by developing an environment of authentic leadership within your organization. Taking action that incorporates proven principles will help your company get from where you are to where you want to be.

The Penny Story

Life Is A Series Of Lessons That

Are Repeated Until Mastered —

And You Will Be Tested

GOING FROM DAY 1 TO DAY 2 OR FROM DAY 30 TO DAY 31 TAKES THE SAME AMOUNT OF EFFORT

Success is about being who you are. It is a journey not a goal — it is not the result of hard work, exacting plans or driving ambition.

1. $.01
2. $.02
3. $.04
4. $.08
5. $.16
6. $.32
7. $.64
8. $1.28
9. $2.56
10. $5.12
11. $10.24
12. $20.48
13. $40.96
14. $81.92
15. $163.84
16. $327.68
17. $655.36
18. $1,310.72
19. $2,621.44
20. $5,242.88
21. $10,485.76
22. $20,971.52
23. $41,943.04
24. $83,886.08
25. $167,772.16
26. $335,544.32
27. $671,088.64
28. $1,342,177.20
29. $2,684,354.40
30. $5,368,708.80
31. $10,737,417.00

THE "OVERNIGHT SUCCESS"

Each of the numbers listed represents a life lesson that you must learn. To go from (1) to (2) does not take any more energy than going from (2) to (3), or from (3) to (4), and so on. By expending the same amount of energy from one level to the next, you eventually reach a "tipping point" where your series of small but steady actions bring you "overnight success." Remember, most "overnight successes" are actually a good ten years in the making!

Note that in order to pass from one level to the next, you must learn the previous day's lesson before you can move on. You will keep getting the same lesson over and over until you have learned it. You will also be tested at each level by the people you love the most. The most important thing is for you to stay the course, remembering that you only have to expend the *same* amount of energy as you move from one level to the next – not more. Your success will result from the accumulation of each lesson you successfully learn.

Want more expertise or a coaching session?
Contact Phil Johnson:

Phil Johnson, MBL Coach

Silicon Synergy Inc

Bus: 905-272-5690

Cell: 416-729-7445

MBLCoach@MasterofBusinessLeadership.com

MasterofBusinessLeadership.com

MasterofBusinessLeadership.blogspot.com

The Power
of Full
Engagement

Energy, not time, is the fundamental currency of
high performance. Good time management skills
are helpful but if we are exhausted to the point of
collapse, what good will a leather bound time plan-
ner do? We do not have a limitless supply of
energy. It is no wonder so many people break
down, burn out, lose their passion.

We live in digital time. Our rhythms are rushed,
rapid fire and relentless, our days carved up into
bits and bytes. We celebrate breadth rather than
depth, quick reaction more than considered reflec-
tion. We skim across the surface, alighting for brief
moments at dozens of destinations but rarely
remaining for long at any one. We race through our

lives without pausing to consider who we really are or where we really want to go. We're wired up but we're melting down. The skilful management of energy, individually and organizationally, makes full engagement possible. To be fully engaged, we must be physically energized, emotionally connected, mentally focused and spiritually aligned with a purpose beyond our immediate self-interest. Being fully engaged means feeling eager to get to work in the morning and just as happy to return home in the evening.

Two Great Lies
We Were Told
Growing Up

*You have to be good
at everything.*

*There is a direct correlation
between effort and results.*

1990–2001

During these years, I did things that I thought I *needed*
to do and *liked* to do.

Gradually, I stopped doing 75% of what I needed
to do, and started doing what I *wanted* to do.

The Way To Your Best Results — YDV × Q
Following Your Energy — An Example

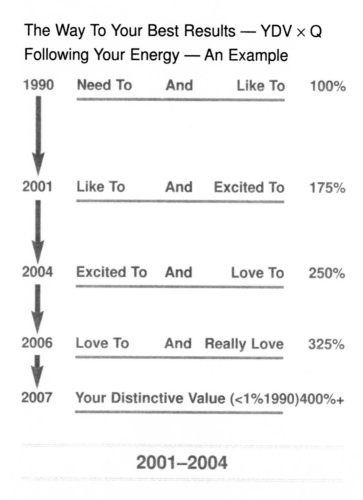

1990	Need To	And	Like To	100%
2001	Like To	And	Excited To	175%
2004	Excited To	And	Love To	250%
2006	Love To	And	Really Love	325%
2007	Your Distinctive Value (<1%1990)			400%+

2001–2004

By 2001, I was doing what I *liked* to do, and what I was *excited* to do.

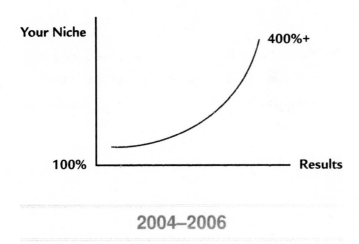

2004–2006

By 2004, I was doing what I was excited to do, and loved to do.

2006

Now, I'm doing what I love to do, and really love to do.

2007

By 2007, I should be doing less than 1% of what I previously did in 1990, 100% of the time. My passion is leadership coaching, which is my "distinctive value," or put another way, my piece of the puzzle.

When You're Green, You Grow — When You're Brown, You Rot

Dr. Carl Jung (1875–1961) proposed that there are four stages of personal growth, development and maturation. They are The Athlete, The Adventurer, The Statesman and The Spiritualist. The Athlete's focus is on the physical world, while the Adventurer concentrates on goals and discovery. The Statesman no longer needs to prove him or herself. He or she seeks to acquire knowledge and wisdom while being of service to others. The Spiritualist has gone beyond the need to be physical, an adventurer or even the need to be intellectual or wise. The Spiritualist's desire is to reconnect with the perfection in each one of us and become interdependent once again. Dr. Jung recognized that we are all interconnected spiritual beings (energy) living a brief physical experience.

Success in business and in life involves finding and staying on your own path as you seek to reconnect with others and achieve synergistic results. Find your own path and refuse any efforts to pull you off. The secret to staying green is in taking action. Focus on the basics and recognize the dramatic changes occurring all around you. There is no such thing as failure. There are only results. Failure is merely a judgment imposed by others. The key is what you do with your results. Abraham Lincoln, Michael Jordan, Tiger Woods, Walt Disney and Thomas Edison failed again and again and again until they succeeded.

The courage you exhibit while moving through your fears, habits and perceptions is the true measure of the importance to you of the desired result.

The Real Competition

Real competition is not a battle about position-based power, assets or revenue. The real war is an internal struggle to be who you truly are as an individual or an organization. In the process of moving through your fears, habits and perceptions, your actions may inspire others (clients, business partners, co-workers) to do the same. This becomes the standard you use to evaluate which activities are essential and which are not — otherwise your decisions tend to be based upon circumstances and pressures at the moment. This generally causes stress, fatigue and conflict.

Being who you are will result in greater resource alignment, revenue, free time and fun. Those that embrace this reality will be the true successes of the 21st Century.

Meeting Phil could not have come at a better time for me. As a new manager I was trying to develop my "management style" but when I started the MBL Program, I soon discovered that being a good manager was not enough. I had to develop my Authentic Leadership and learn that I am perfect! Phil's coaching has allowed me to re-focus and be much more strategic in managing my piece of the business which is already paying dividends. That being said however, the most rewarding part of Phil's coaching is that I can apply it to all aspects of my life, not just in business, which makes the MBL Program different from the other management ideologies I have come across over the years. The world is evolving and role-based leadership is becoming a thing of the past and I am excited to be in the forefront of the new age of Authentic Leadership!

— Pino Biase, VP Business Development

Becoming
A Trimtab
YDY × Q

> *A large ship goes by, and then comes the rudder. On the edge of the rudder is a miniature rudder called a trimtab. Moving that trimtab builds a low pressure which turns the rudder that steers the gigantic ship with almost no effort. One individual can be a trimtab, making a major difference.*
> — Buckminster Fuller, 1895–1983

If we look to see where we can make the most difference with the least effort, we will be able to do much more with very little ... we will be a trimtab.

You can choose to make the rest of your life
the best of your life — it's all about you!

Want more expertise or a coaching session?
Contact Phil Johnson:

Phil Johnson, MBL Coach

Silicon Synergy Inc

Bus: 905-272-5690

Cell: 416-729-7445

MBLCoach@MasterofBusinessLeadership.com

MasterofBusinessLeadership.com

MasterofBusinessLeadership.blogspot.com

Future Vision

Creating A Vision For Your Life That Goes Beyond Your Life!

Creating a vision for your life that goes beyond your life connects your present actions not only with current but also future generations. This vision can be a source of courage for you to move through your fears, habits and perceptions.

Instead of looking backward, creating a vision of a compelling "bigger future" will provide you with the energy and clarity to make decisions. There is no such thing as failure there are only results. "Failure" is simple a judgment imposed by others. The key is what will you do with your results? What have you learned?

What's next?

The results of your authentic leadership will be understood and have its greatest impact on generations yet to be born. Great leaders from past generations have known this truth.

What We Do In This Present Moment Matters

45

2,000

100,000

4,000,000

200,000,000

10,000,000,000

Employee
Talent

It is talent, not physical capital that drives financial performance in the new economy. Yet today's
annual reports are still full of facts and figures
derived from metrics geared to 20th Century
industrial management models. The principal
source of information we use to measure business
success today is a backward view based on a dou-
ble-entry accounting technique invented by the
Italians 600 years ago.

In the 21st Century economy the true source of
corporate wealth are intangibles. It's the knowledge, relationships, reputations and services
created by talented people. More than 75 percent
of wealth created today is service related. For
example, car manufacturers make more money
from providing financial services than from manu-

facturing cars. The intangible capital of the world's largest 150 companies has been estimated at $7.5 trillion - up from $800 billion just a decade ago.

So why do companies continue to gauge their performance by measuring returns on invested capital rather than the contributions made by talented people? Leadership development, knowledge creation, research and development and so forth are almost always expensed on a "What can we afford?" basis. Maybe it's because we aren't measuring (and therefore investing in) what really matters. The clock has run out on workforce development investment strategies that stopped being effective a long time ago.

Review

Tools, Tips And Insights

"ONE-A-DAYS"

1. Be who you are and inspire others to do the same. That is the single underlying truth in this book and in life. True leadership is not about changing who you are — it's about being who you are.

2. Allow yourself to be a truly authentic leader, one who has the ability to arouse "discretionary energy" in others. This form of leadership serves to inspire individuals to want to contribute more. As a leader, you inspire others to become leaders instead of operating in the old 20th Century position-based power model.

3. Find the courage to view your own current reality. You are likely to discover an urgent need and energy to move in the direction of better results. You take action and, in the process, confront the fears, habits, and perceptions standing in your way.

4. Embrace the idea that leadership comes from somewhere inside you. It is *not* simply something you do. It is a process, an expression of who you are. At its deepest level, *leadership is authentic self-expression that creates value.* This is YDV × Q — your distinctive value times the quantity of people affected.

5. Ask yourself *"What am I going to do with the time I have left?"* This is an important question no matter how long you have to live.

6. Acknowledge and move through your fears. The stories you tell yourself begin to change when you take action.

7. Accept that leaders come in all shapes and sizes. The truly authentic leader is a Servant Warrior. Each is a unique blend of personal humility and professional will.

8. Take action. It requires both trust and a willingness to take risk. Risk is involved because many times the end result is not

visible without first taking the action. Taking action requires acknowledging and moving through fears.

9. Listen to the stories you tell yourself. Those stories may be coloring your views. The stories begin to change when you take action.

10. Keep a low profile while staying on top of trends and developments. Take small, almost-invisible action on issues before they grow into problems. Invisible leaders are the unsung heroes who are building your organization's future one small brick at a time.

11. Realize that life is simply a series of interconnected moments. It is action that makes the connections.

12. Create a niche for your organization by delivering a quality product or service. The smaller the niche, the bigger the market. At this point the market becomes the marketer.

13. Look at the new wealth of the 21st Century in people, not money or things. The industrial control model of the 20th Century treats chairs, buildings, and land as assets, and people as expenses. People are the true assets.

14. View leadership as a choice, not a position. Unleash rather than liquidate the human potential within people. Move from the "quick-fix" exterior (outside-in) approach to a sequential internal (inside-out) approach.

15. Remember that people are your number one asset. The development of people, more than any other activity, is at the heart of business growth.

16. Realize the ultimate 21st Century product and service is you and your intellectual property. The more you are able to develop and package your unique "IP" the greater your potential market. As you become your market niche, your market becomes global.

17. Consider that the most efficient use of available resources, the fastest time-to-market, and the greatest profitability occur when your company's success and your client's success become interdependent. It is at this point you realize your mutual business relationship has become a critically important component of your organization's ultimate success.

18. Notice when people within an organization are in consensus, their various tasks and activities auto-

matically operate in alignment. Faster time-to-market and better resource utilization are just a few of the potential benefits.

19. Realize that today's global economy requires quick and correct decisions. The natural human instinct is to slow down or avoid making decisions when the stakes are as high as they are today. You may want more information and need more time instead of acting quickly and correctly. Refusing to recognize and respond to change rapidly will severely hamper your company's ability to succeed.

20. Learn to ask others for their input. Leaders in the 21st Century are learning how to "ask." Asking for input and ideas takes courage. You have that courage within you.

21. Say "thank you" when you've gotten someone's input. Then STOP, think, and feel. Manage any immediate urge you have to give your opinion of their ideas. Keep any eventual feedback positive, simple, and focused.

22. Recognize and applaud any individuals willing to challenge themselves to develop their leadership. Be part of the local businesses and governments that support and encourage individuals to develop

their leadership to compete within the global economy.

23. Look at the thoughts, opinions, and actions of others more objectively, without taking things personally. It is the best way to become a better listener. It is not easy to do yet it is very do-able.

24. Recognize that the first direction a seed grows in the ground is inward and downward, to develop a strong root system. A seed cannot sustain its life if it grows upward and forward first. Corporations often push to move forward without the proper internal alignment or adequate foundation.

25. Create the environment where success can be achieved. You are not responsible for an individual's personal success. Taking that responsibility from them robs the person of their opportunity to deal with the issues and circumstances that stand in the way of their own growth.

26. Realize that *Growth* and *Bigness* are different. Bigness is ultimately not sustainable. Customer relationships become less important and growth slows down. Bigness prompts a company's inward focus. Growth comes from developing resources to their full potential.

27. Challenge your employees to go beyond where they think they can go. Through coaching, they are able to see themselves or a situation in a fresh, new way. Coaching uses a process and a system that delivers individual growth, purposeful action, and sustained improvement.

28. Understand that employees are longing for leaders they can trust. Spirituality is an emerging mega trend and is surprisingly practical in business. Its absence can lead to arrogance, greed, and mistrust.

29. Become immune to others' thoughts, opinions, and actions. You then become more focused, relaxed, connected, effective, and happy. This does not mean that you give up responsibility for your actions. It means you stop taking responsibility for and reacting to the actions of others.

30. Develop authentic leadership as something good for both your business and your health. The need for balance has been recognized as a way of avoiding *dis-ease* from at least as far back as the time of Aristotle. Illness was thought to arise from being out of balance. The same can be said about dysfunctional organizations.

Oseola McCarty, 1908–1999

Leadership In Action!
An Authentic Leader Just "Doing What Needs Doing"
Inspirational Servant-Warrior, Trimtab, Fully Engaged,
An Invisible Leader — Teaching People To Fish

1908–1995

Oseola McCarty died on September 27, 1999 in Hattiesburg, a town in Mississippi, in the southern United States. She was 91 years old. Although she was a small,

delicate woman, Oseola had worked hard as a washer-
woman all her life. She took in clothes for laundering
and ironing from many people in the town. She seldom
left her small house except to go to church or to buy
groceries. She always saved money, a dollar or two at a
time, and by the time she was 87 she had over $250,000 in
the bank. Because she was getting close to the end of her
life and didn't need the money for anything, she decided
to give almost all of it away. She used $150,000 to
establish a scholarship fund to help poor students in
Mississippi get a university education. Even though she
had made the gift in preparation for death, Oseola's generosity threw her into a life that was very different from
the one she had been leading for so long.

1995–1999 THE "OVERNIGHT SUCCESS"

Oseola quickly became famous. She was honoured by the
United Nations. She shook hands with Bill Clinton and
received the Presidential Citizen's Medal from him.
She received an honorary doctorate from Harvard
University. In 1996, she carried the Olympic torch

through part of Mississippi. And in the same year she flicked the switch that dropped the ball in New York City's New Year's Eve celebration. It was the first time in her life she had stayed up past midnight. The American public loved Oseola. At airports, admirers always surrounded her and people reached out to touch her as she went by. Although she had not expected this sort of attention, she enjoyed it very much. Her generosity inspired over 600 other people to make contributions totalling $330,000 to the fund. When Ted Turner heard about what she had done, he made a personal contribution to the United Nations of $1 Billion.

Leaders Come In All Shapes And Sizes And Can Arouse "Discretionary Energy" In Others

Leadership Performance - What is it?

Why bother? According to Gallup's Annual Employee Engagement Index the 2006 level of workforce engagement was 29%. Employee engagement was defined as "a heightened emotional connection that an employee feels for his or her organization, that influences him or her to exert greater discretionary effort to his or her work." In 2006 alone the lack of employee engagement was estimated to have cost the United States $350 Billion; Canada $35 Billion; France 100 Billion Euros; and the United Kingdom $64 Billion.

The research overwhelmingly confirms authentic leadership can make a huge difference in business results. It can arouse "discretionary energy" in others. The management of people based upon position power has continually been proven to be far less effective.

Employee compensation is one of the largest investments firms make each year. Would you like a higher level of workforce engagement leading to better results?

Protect your investment by establishing an authentic leadership development program. Give your people the tools and insights they need to succeed. Help them become true servant warrior leaders and watch your business become more prosperous via an engaged workforce.

Want more expertise or a coaching session?
Contact Phil Johnson:

Phil Johnson, MBL Coach

Silicon Synergy Inc

Bus: 905-272-5690

Cell: 416-729-7445

MBLCoach@MasterofBusinessLeadership.com

MasterofBusinessLeadership.com

MasterofBusinessLeadership.blogspot.com

Final Comments

A large ship goes by, and then comes the rudder. On the edge of the rudder is a miniature rudder called a trimtab. Moving that trimtab builds a low pressure which turns the rudder that steers the gigantic ship with almost no effort. One individual can be a trimtab, making a major difference.

If we look to see where we can make the most difference with the least effort we will be able to do much more with very little ... we will be a trimtab.

The things to do are the things that need doing that you see need to be done.
— Buckminster Fuller, 1895—1983

Take extremely good care of yourself every day.

This is where leadership begins. The development of authentic leaders is one of the greatest challenges of the 21st Century. To live a life that reflects more of you — your values and deepest desires. In today's world most people live with a sense that something is missing. We have lost part of ourselves in the daily madness of our busy lives.

You are perfect — there is nothing missing.

The ultimate goal in business and in life is the same. To be who you are and in the process of being who you are inspire others to be who they are. This can and will create consensus, alignment, interdependence, interconnectedness and a global synergy.

You are what you think and what you think comes from your actions. Do not worry about doing your best. Just take action and the story you tell yourself will begin to change. Complete understanding can only come from the actions you take. Your desire to serve others with humility and courage will keep you on the path to becoming a *Master of Business Leadership*!

Between stimulus and response is a space. In this space lies the freedom to choose our response. In these choices lie our growth and our happiness. Next to life itself, this awareness and our freedom to choose, to direct our lives, is our most precious gift and power.

Action > Leader/Victim Awareness/Choice
> Individual And Organizational Healing

About
The Author

Phil Johnson is a Master of Business Leadership
Coach. He was born in Ontario, Canada in 1953.
During Phil's 25-year career in the semiconductor
industry he led several successful companies while trav-
elling throughout North America and the Pacific Rim.
He graduated from McMaster University's DeGroote
School of Business in 1978. He went on to study
Electrical Engineering. Corporate roles as Vice President
and Director of World Wide Sales were declined so that
he could establish the Master of Business Leadership
program. Phil and his wife Brenda live in
Mississauga, Ontario, Canada.

You Are Perfect!
(Really)

The search for external power has created the fear that sets individuals and corporations against each other. It is the same struggle that creates conflict and wars. It is the same struggle that set Cain against Abel. All of our social, economic and political institutions reflect our understanding of power as external. We are in a time of deep change. We will move through this change more easily if we are conscious of the road on which we are traveling, our destination and what it is that is in motion.

By developing our authentic leadership we connect with our internal power as individuals and organizations leading to greater alignment and synergistic results. You are perfect (really). Our habits, fears and perceptions have created the "walls" that blind us to our perfection. We have evolved as far as intellect will take us. As a species, we are moving from the view and pursuit of power and leadership as external to the pursuit of authentic internal power and leadership. We are becoming consciousness of our perfection.

You can choose to make this year a launching pad for the rest of your life. Take extremely good care of yourself every day. This is where leadership begins. To live a life that reflects more of you, your values and deepest desires. In today's world, many people live with a sense that something is missing. You feel that you have lost part of yourself in the daily madness of your busy life. You are perfect. There is nothing missing. The rest of your life can be the best of your life. It's your choice — it always has been.

Manor House Publishing
www.manor-house.biz
905 648 2193

CPSIA information can be obtained
at www.ICGtesting.com
Printed in the USA
LVOW12*0408110717

540939LV00002B/22/P